Narrowboat Holidays

GW00371056

- **SUPERB BOATS**
- **WIDE CHOICE OF ROUTES**
- **ONE-WAY TRIPS**
- **SHORT BREAKS**
- **CRUISE THE STOURPORT RING, AVON RING OR THE MAGNIFICENT LLANGOLLEN CANAL**
- **BASES AT WORCESTER AND WHITCHURCH**

TELEPHONE 0905 28667 FOR YOUR *FREE* COLOUR BROCHURE

Anglo Welsh Waterway Holidays

THE MARKET LEADERS
110 BOATS FROM 6 BASES

Specialists in waterway short breaks and
one-way cruises on Canals and Rivers
throughout the country.

Phone or write for a brochure today
ANGLO WELSH WATERWAY HOLIDAYS
10 Canal Basin, Market Harborough,
Leicester LE16 7BJ.

Telephone No. 0858 466910.
Fax No. 0858 434618.

Pearson's Canal Companion
SHROPSHIRE UNION
& LLANGOLLEN CANALS

Published by J. M. Pearson & Son,
Tatenhill Common, Burton-on-Trent, Staffordshire   DE13 9RS
Telephone (0283) 713674

© Michael Pearson. All rights reserved.

Third edition 1989. Revised 1990/91. ISBN 0 907864 51 1

Maps by Malcolm Barnes Cartographer of Burton upon Trent.

Typeset by Character Graphics of Taunton, Somerset.

Printed by Penwell of Callington, Cornwall.

Introduction

THE Llangollen Canal and Shropshire Union Canal are two of the most scenically beautiful inland waterways in Great Britain. Although now considered as separate entities, historically they were both part of the once extensive Shropshire Union system which also included the Montgomery Canal, the subject of an ambitious restoration scheme.

THESE days the Llangollen and Shropshire Union canals offer 120 miles of rewarding recreational amenity for boaters, walkers, anglers and general visitors. One of the most interesting facets of these waterways is the contrast in style brought about by the divergence in period of the constituent canals. What we now call the Shropshire Union is made up of the Chester Canal of 1779, the Wirral Line of the Ellesmere Canal opened in 1795, and the Birmingham & Liverpool Junction Canal dating from 1835. The Llangollen Canal was equally fragmented in its construction, being part of an ambitious plan to link the rivers Dee and Severn which never came to fruition.

EQUAL variety is displayed in the landscapes traversed by the two canals: from the levels of the Wirral and the mosses west of Whitchurch, through the rolling farmlands of the Shropshire/Staffordshire border, to the secretive charm of the Shropshire meres and the dramatic majesty of the Welsh mountains.

IN this 3rd, completely revised, edition of the Pearson Canal Companion to the Llangollen & Shropshire Union all the maps have been redrawn to new standards which we feel have both improved clarity and enhanced visual appeal. Coverage has been increased to include the Trent & Mersey Canal between Middlewich and Anderton, both for boaters commencing their cruise from that area and those visiting the historic Anderton Lift from bases on the Llangollen or Shropshire Union canals. The commentary has been considerably rewritten and extended and all photography is now in full colour. We sincerely hope that past users will welcome these improvements and that newcomers will be impressed by the standard and content of this Canal Companion. If you have constructive comments please do not hesitate to contact us. In the meantime we wish you much enjoyment from your exploration of these splendid canals.

Despite the proximity of Wolverhampton, Autherley, like many canal junctions, is self-contained. It is not pretty in a conventional way, being bordered by housing estates, waterworks and public open spaces. The old boatmen called it 'Cut End' for the obvious reason that the Shropshire Union Canal began and ended here. Once there was all the paraphernalia of a meeting of waterways: toll office, stables, workshops, employees cottages, and a dominant, sweeping roving bridge carrying the Staffs & Worcs towpath over the entrance to the Shropshire Union; a stop lock protected the two companies precious water supplies. Much of this infrastructure remains, enjoying a new lease of life in the leisure age as a hire base and boatyard.

Nowadays the cast of boats may have altered, but Autherley's dramatic significance remains, and pleasure boaters have a choice of routes: South-west to Stourport and the river Severn; South-east via the adjacent (and not to be confused) *Aldersley Junction* to Wolverhampton and the lugubrious waters of the BCN; North-east to Great Haywood and the Trent & Mersey; North-west to Nantwich and beyond. And it is this final route upon which we concentrate here, soon shaking off the suburbs and, beyond bridge 4, encountering a rolling, empty countryside, so characteristic of 'The Shroppie'.

Navigational Note
The channel narrows briefly south of bridges 5 and 6 and there is insufficent room for boats to pass each other.

Autherley Junction

Eating & Drinking
There are pubs on the housing estates, but thirsty canallers are likely to prefer the licensed club house at Water Travel's boatyard. Visitors are also welcomed at Wolverhampton Boat Club.

Shopping
Again, shops and supermarkets on the housing estates, but much handier is the range of frozen foods and general groceries obtainable at Water Travel's shop beside the stop lock.

Public Transport
BUSES - frequent services into Wolverhampton from bridges 65 and 62A. Tel: Wolverhampton (0902) 51676.
TRAINS - Wolverhampton is a major railhead. Details on W. 59545.

Boatyards & Hire Bases
WATER TRAVEL – Oxley Moor Road, Wolverhampton, West Mids. Tel: Wolverhampton (0902) 782371. 2 to 8 berth hire craft (Hoseasons). Pumpout, diesel, petrol, gas, slipway, lift-out and storage, boatbuilding & brokerage, repairs & servicing, short-term moorings, shop, payphone and toilets.
OXLEY MOOR STOP – adjacent bridge 65. Tel: (0902) 789522. Pumpout, diesel, gas, gifts and provisions.

* Estimated time refers to bridges 1-7 section only.

THE SHROPSHIRE UNION CANAL slices through the Staffordshire countryside in cuttings and upon embankments typical of the bold, 19th century designs of Thomas Telford, who engineered this route between Autherley and Nantwich, originally known as the Birmingham & Liverpool Junction Canal. Travelling northwards you rapidly become attuned to the unique atmosphere of this canal. Far from becoming monotonous, its purposeful, loping stride across the landscape seems to engender a strange exhilarance, intensified by the recurring contrast of shadowy cuttings and panorama providing embankments; known as 'rockings' and 'valleys' respectively to past generations of boatmen.

There are two notable structures either side of Brewood. To the south the distinctly ornate, balustraded Avenue Bridge (No.10) carries the carriageway to Chillington Hall. The advent of canals heralded many similar attempts at ornamentation and disguise, where powerful landowners would only grant permission for a waterway to cross their parklands if suitable steps were taken to adorn the otherwise purely functional architecture of the new trade route. In contrast, north of Brewood, the canal crosses the old Roman Road of Watling Street on a sturdy, yet elegant aqueduct of iron, brick and stone construction, inscribed 1832. Canal travellers, be they on foot (the towpath here being part of the 'Staffordshire Way') or afloat, can gaze down with a very real sense of superiority on the traffic of the A5, in full knowledge that their's is the older, wiser mode of transport.

Brewood

A lovely village, once a small town, retaining an ancient air of calm, doubtless because it had the luck to be ignored by the A5, and later the M54. The natives call it 'Brood' and there really is a timelessness about it which seduces you into spending longer here than you might have planned. Winding lanes of gracious houses lead to the old market place where the archaic vehicles of the Green Bus Co pause before rumbling off to Wolverhampton and Cannock. Occasionally they still operate 'half-cab' double deckers whose conductors still sell tickets from a rack of many colours; instant nostalgia! Enhancing one corner of the square is 'Speedwell Castle', a Gothick fantasy erected in the 18th century with the winnings on a racehorse called Speedwell. Within cycling distance to the west lies Boscobel House, where Charles II was hidden in an oak tree.

Eating & Drinking

ADMIRAL RODNEY – (1). Effectively refurbished by Holt, Plant & Deakin (the Black Country brewers) in 'Victorian Parlour' style. Good bar meals, families catered for. Garden with playground.

SWAN HOTEL – Market Square. Bass and bar lunches; friendly village local.

LAVELLES – Church Street. Informal restaurant. Bookings on Brewood 850989 Or 850001.

Shopping

Old fashioned shops where you can eavesdrop on local gossip including: baker, butcher, delicatessen, chemist, newsagent and post office. Also a supermarket and a branch of Lloyds Bank.

Places to Visit

CHILLINGTON HALL – 1½ miles west of bridge 10. Open Thursdays, May to mid September, and Sundays in August, 2.30 – 5.30pm. Admission charge. Georgian House with landscaped grounds by Capability Brown.

Public Transport

BUSES – splendid Green Bus Co services on an hourly basis (Mon-Sat) to/from Wolverhampton. Some run through to/from Wheaton Aston and are useful for one-way towpath walks. Also occasional services to Penkridge and Cannock. Tel: Cheslyn Hay (0922) 414141 for timetable information.

Boatyard & Hire Base

COUNTRYWIDE CRUISERS – Brewood, Staffs ST19 9BG. Tel: Brewood (0902) 850166. 4 to 8 berth hire craft (Blue Riband Club). Pumpout, Elsan disposal, diesel, water, repairs & servicing, slipway, gas, moorings and shop.

WHEATON ASTON LOCK is strangely solitary - the only one in 25 miles of canal; a telling statistic of Telford's engineering. For about a mile the canal penetrates the deciduous heart of Lapley wood and there's another typical Shroppie cutting by Little Onn, but elsewhere the embankments offer wide views eastwards towards Cannock Chase.

How astonishingly remote and unpeopled the landscape seems. The West Midlands conurbation is less than a dozen miles to the south, yet moor for the night between Wheaton Aston and Little Onn, and you'll have only the occasional eerie hoot of a hunting owl or the distant silent wash of headlights on a country lane for company.

Abandoned wartime aerodromes inevitably have their ghosts and in decay accumulate a patina of lore and legend, hard perhaps to equate with the often mundane use to which they were put after closure. Wheaton Aston was opened in 1941 and became one of the RAF's largest training units, operating a squadron of 'Oxfords'. It was by all accounts an unenviable posting, there being little in the way of entertainment for off-duty pilots and ground staff. There were however occasional dramas. Once a visiting American 'Thunderbolt' crash-landed in the canal. Another well remembered wartime incident occurred at the lock when a narrowboat, carrying an unsheeted cargo of shining aluminium on a moonlit night, was attacked by a German aircraft which unleashed a bomb that exploded less than a hundred yards from the chamber. After the war the aerodrome was abandoned in 1947 and subsequently became a pig farm.

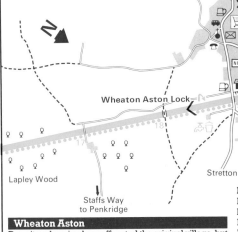

Wheaton Aston

Dormitory housing has suffocated the original village, but people have to live somewhere and the 'incomers' natter on their way to and from the shops much as the farm wives would have done when this was solely a farming community. No, this is no picture postcard village, but after its late 20th century fashion it's a village alive and kicking, and therefore arguably more justifiable than a village pretty but pickled.

Eating & Drinking
HARTLEY ARMS – canalside bridge 19. Friendly and neat little pub serving Banks's and bar snacks.
LA CALVADOS – ½ mile west of bridge 13 in village. French restaurant open Tue-Sat for dinner and on Sunday for lunch. Tel: W.A. (0785) 840707 for bookings.

Shopping
Post office, general stores, baker, butchers, newsagents and grocers 5 minutes from canal at bridge 19. Most shops close for lunch. Turner's garage by bridge 19 stocks Calor gas, diesel and boating accessories.

Public Transport
BUSES - regular but not frequent services to/from Brewood, Wolverhampton, Penkridge & Cannock. Contact: Green Bus Co on Cheslyn Hay (0922) 414141.

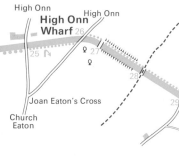

DEEP, SHADOWY SANDSTONE cuttings, spanned by lichened grey stone bridges of simple balance and unaffected beauty, lead to the eighty-one unlined yards of Cowley Tunnel; the only one on the Shropshire Union. Once a dizzy jungle of trees darkened the approaches so much that you were never quite sure where the tunnel began and the cutting ended, but their roots caused instabilities in what was already a brittle rock strata (Telford, and his contractor William Provis, had intended the tunnel to be much longer) and they were felled in 1985, leaving the cutting seeming strangely bare to those who had known it before.

On a clear day the embankments north of Gnosall reveal that famous Shropshire landmark, The Wrekin, 15 miles to the south-west; a slumbering hunchback of a summit, 1335ft high. A.E. Housman immortalised it in 'A Shropshire Lad', and Salopians raise their glasses 'To all friends around the Wrekin'.

The dismantled railway line which crossed the canal at Gnosall once usefully connected Stafford with Shrewsbury until a certain Doctor made his presence felt. Historically it was unusual in that it was actually built by the Shropshire Union Canal Company, apparently hedging their bets on the transport mode of the future. When, in 1846, they leased themselves to the London & North Western Railway, there can have been few shareholders who would have backed the canal to outlast the railway as it has done.

Gnosall Heath

This appendage of Gnosall grew up with the coming of the canal. Two pubs slaked the thirst of passing boatmen, a steam powered flour mill took advantage of the new transport mode, and a non-conformist chapel kept a sense of proportion amidst all the excitement. Nowadays the pubs pander to boaters and passing motorists, the flour mill has become an attractive private residence, and the chapel is a hardware store. Gnosall itself lies half a mile or so to the east; pleasant enough, but hardly compelling unless you have an enthusiasm for church architecture, for the parish church is substantial and largely 13th century. Oh, and by the way, you don't pronounce the 'G'!

Eating & Drinking

THE BOAT - bridge 34. Well known canal pub with curiously attractive curved wall abutting the bridge. Marstons, bar meals, bar billiards and pleasant garden by the water's edge.

THE NAVIGATION - bridge 35. Courage, lunches and garden with childrens playground.

Fish & chips open Wed-Sat lunch and Mon-Sat evenings.

Shopping

General store (open Sun am), newsagent and butcher by bridge 34; plus bakery further along Wharf Road towards Gnosall itself. Co-op store (open Sun am) and post office by bridge 35. Small branch of Barclays in Gnosall.

Public Transport

BUSES - Happy Days services to/from Stafford and Newport, hourly Mon-Sat. Tel: Woodseaves (078 574) 231. *Newport is an interesting old town with a good range of shops and refreshments. Remains of the former Norbury - Shrewsbury canal can be seen. Journey time by bus, 10 minutes; by bicycle, 30 minutes.*

A MASK OF TALL trees disguises the immensity of Shelmore embankment. It was six years in the making and, in its way, was as glorious an engineering feat as any of Telford's more visibly imposing aqueducts. A vast army of navvies and horses were employed on it. Spoil from the big cuttings at nearby Gnosall and Grub Street was brought by wagon for its construction. To Telford's dismay the earthworks slipped time after time and, as the rest of the canal was finished, Shelmore stubbornly refused to hold. In poor health, Telford struggled to oversee its completion, conscious that the bank need not have been tackled at all had

Lord Anson of Norbury Park sanctioned the preferred course through Shelmore Wood. Perhaps we should regard his lordship more kindly from the perspective of the 20th century where environmentalists, protecting the landscape from the intrusion of new motorways, are deemed to be on the side of the angels.

North of Norbury Junction lies Grub Street cutting. For over a mile the canal is wrapped in a thick coat of vegetation, again, like Shelmore, hiding the sheer size of the of the eighty feet deep cutting. At the southern end of the cutting the A519 crosses the canal on an unusual double-arched bridge which supports a tiny telegraph pole, a survivor from the line which once marched beside the Shroppie for much of its length. A black, monkey-like creature is reputed to have haunted this bridge since a boatman was drowned here in the 19th century, and, indeed, spectres seem tangible enough passing through Grub Street at dusk.

Sadly, Norbury is no longer a 'junction', though the name lives on. How nice it would be now to lock down the 'Seventeen Steps' of the Newport Branch and head across the marshy emptiness of Shropshire's Weald Moors to Shrewsbury; encountering Telford's early cast iron aqueduct at Longdon-on-Tern and the 970 yard Berwick Tunnel.

Norbury Junction

Though the suffix is misleading these days, Norbury is still a flourishing canal centre where British Waterways have an office and a maintenance yard. This is home for a fleet of dredgers and work boats which keep sections of the Shropshire Union and Staffordshire & Worcestershire canals in as good a state of upkeep as the budget will allow. Built purely as a canal community, one or two of the houses are still inhabited by waterway staff, but three are available for holiday let through the boatyard. Indeed, Norbury attracts land based visitors like a magnet and, mindful of their potential as boating holidaymakers, the local hire base operates day and trip boat services to whet the appetite for canal cruises of lengthier duration.

Eating & Drinking

THE MEASHAM TEAPOT – cosy little adjunct to the boatyard shop. Named after the celebrated pottery ware which emanated from the Ashby Canal in Leicestershire and found favour with working boat families. Light meals and refreshments usually available during the cruising season.

THE JUNCTION INN – canalside. Busy, but not brash pub with lots of facilities: Banks's beers, bar and restaurant meals, familes catered for, large garden with good children's play area.

THE ANCHOR – canalside bridge 42. Delightfully unspoilt boatman's pub. Various 'real ales', including bitter from the independent Oak Brewery of Manchester served fresh from the barrel in the cellar. Sandwiches to order. Nice old fashioned garden separated from the towpath by a privet hedge.

Shopping

Provisions from the boatyard shop. Small crafts outlet in the pub garden. No shops in Norbury village.

Boatyard & Hire Base

SHROPSHIRE UNION CRUISES – Norbury Junction, Stafford ST20 0PN. Tel: Stafford (0785) 74292. 2 to 12 berth hire craft (Blakes), bookings through Dartline of Bunbury on (0829) 260638. Pumpout, diesel, petrol, moorings, repairs & servicing, drydock, slipway, chandlery, gift shop and payphone. Day boats for hire and holiday cottages to let.

CROSSING THE BORDER between Staffordshire and Shropshire, the canal continues to traverse an unruffled landscape of prosperous farms; an extraordinarily remote region, one is tempted to categorise as 'lost' but for the obvious truth that it had never been 'found' in the first place. Country roads, largely innocent of traffic, cross the canal but rarely run parallel to it, defying easy exploration of 'The Shroppie' in a motor car.

At KNIGHTON one comes suddenly upon a disconcertingly large factory. It seems intrusive, amidst these rolling pastures, until you discover that it was opened by Cadburys, the chocolate manufacturers, in 1911 as a centre for the processing of milk collected from the dairy farming hinterland of the Shropshire Union Canal. Canal transport was used exclusively to bring countless churns gathered from numerous wharves along the canal; that at High Onn (Map 4) being a fine example. Cadburys operated their own distinctive fleet of narrowboats, being one of the first operators to experiment with motorised craft. Cocoa and sugar were also brought by boat to Knighton and blended with milk to make 'crumb', a sort of raw chocolate, which was subsequently taken to Bournville, again by boat, to be transformed into the finished delicacy.

The last boatman regularly to trade here was the famous Charlie Atkins senior; nicknamed 'Chocolate Charlie' for obvious reasons. He carried the final cargo of crumb from Knighton to Bournville aboard the narrowboat *Mendip* in 1961, since when all transport to and from the works has inevitably and somewhat sadly been by road; though the wharf remains incongruously well maintained, as if the last consignment had been despatched just days ago. Nowadays the factory belongs to the Premier Beverage Products Company, its main activities being the manufacture of powdered milk and cocoa.

Apart from the Cadbury connection, Knighton's claim to fame dates from 1660, when Charles II granted a special Act of Parliament absolving its inhabitants from the need to pay rates. This munificent concession held good right up until the introduction of the Poll Tax.

The sleepy village of CHESWARDINE lies about a mile to the east of bridge 53 – it can also be reached from Goldstone Wharf – see Map 7. The walk is uphill but worthwhile, for there are two pubs, a post office and general stores and a butcher. Billingtons manufacture gingerbread in the village (on sale at the shop) and the church is particularly fine.

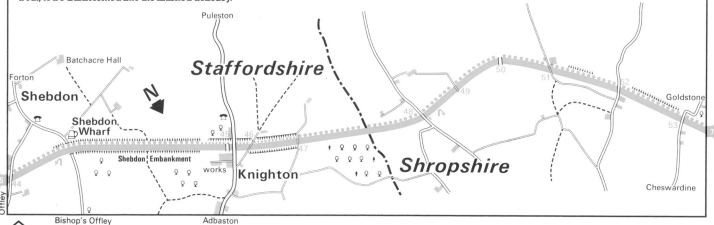

THE SHROPPIE FLIRTS with the county boundary, the towpath itself forming the actual demarcation from bridge 58 to 62, so that technically the canal lies briefly in Staffordshire. The landscape, though, is impervious to the machinations of local government, remaining aloof and typically remote: a tall, dark, silent canal, this Shropshire Union.

WOODSEAVES is another prodigious cutting, at points almost a hundred feet deep. These cuttings proved just as troublesome to Telford as the embankments. There were frequent avalanches during construction and, even today, lumps of brittle sandstone are inclined to dislodge themselves and tumble into the canal. British Waterways are undertaking a rolling programme of remedial work to bolster the inherent instabilities of the cutting. A feature of Woodseaves is its high bridges, spanning the canal like portals to the mysterious chasms of another world.

At TYRLEY a flight of five locks – the last to be faced southbound for seventeen miles – carry the canal down into, or up out of, Market Drayton. The lower chambers are located in a shadowy sandstone cutting across which branches intertwine to form a tunnel of trees. Damp and rarely touched by direct sunlight, all manner of mosses and ferns flourish in this conducive environment. After dusk, bats leave their tree hole roosts to hunt for insects, acrobatically twisting and turning over the luminous pounds between the locks. The well surfaced towpath makes the flight popular with pedestrians, though there are no formal parking facilities on the lane which crosses the canal at bridge 60. The provision of water, sanitary station and rubbish points above the top lock satisfies the needs of boaters too, making Tyrley a gregarious overnight mooring spot.

TYRLEY WHARF was a point of discharge and collection for the local estate at Peatswood; presumably the usual sort of commodities: coal in, agricultural produce out. The buildings date from 1837 and were erected in a graceful Tudor style. Nowadays, its commercial significance a thing of the dim and distant past, it would be difficult to imagine a more picturesque scene. The lock cottage is of typical Telford design, there are similar structures at Audlem and Wheaton Aston, and there is a definite family resemblance to the toll houses on the London – Holyhead road which Telford also designed.

Regular travellers along 'The Shroppie' will be disappointed that Ken and Lillias Greenhalgh have had to close their popular Waterside Crafts shop. Happily though, the couple continue to live in Tyrley and what was the shop has been transformed into an idyllic self-catering cottage: bookings and further details are available on Market Drayton (0630) 4228.

Navigational Advice
A 2mph speed limit is in force through Woodseaves Cutting, and boaters should take extreme care passing oncoming craft in the narrowest sections.

Eating & Drinking
THE WHARF TAVERN – canalside at Goldstone Wharf (bridge 55). One of the Shroppie's most popular inns, 'The Wharf' is a free house (Ansells, Stones & Tartan bitters) widely regarded for its restaurant meals. Bar food – including an ample summer buffet – is also available. There is a canalside garden with children's play area and a payphone on the premises.
THE FOUR ALLS – situated on A529, ½ mile west of Tyrley top lock. Country house motel open 'all day'. Bar and restaurant meals usually available. Tel: Market Drayton 2995.

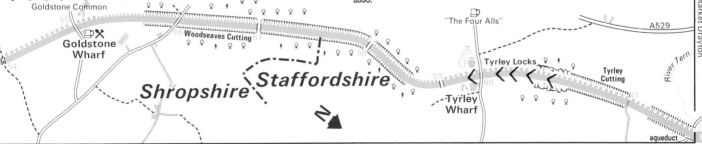

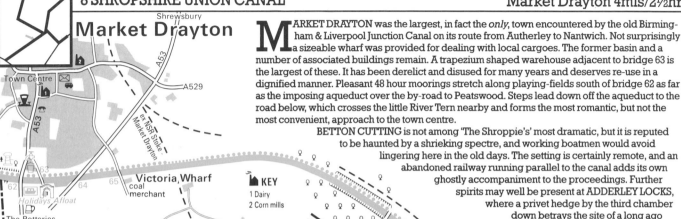

Market Drayton

M ARKET DRAYTON was the largest, in fact the *only*, town encountered by the old Birmingham & Liverpool Junction Canal on its route from Autherley to Nantwich. Not surprisingly a sizeable wharf was provided for dealing with local cargoes. The former basin and a number of associated buildings remain. A trapezium shaped warehouse adjacent to bridge 63 is the largest of these. It has been derelict and disused for many years and deserves re-use in a dignified manner. Pleasant 48 hour moorings stretch along playing-fields south of bridge 62 as far as the imposing aqueduct over the by-road to Peatswood. Steps lead down off the aqueduct to the road below, which crosses the little River Tern nearby and forms the most romantic, but not the most convenient, approach to the town centre.

BETTON CUTTING is not among 'The Shroppie's' most dramatic, but it is reputed to be haunted by a shrieking spectre, and working boatmen would avoid lingering here in the old days. The setting is certainly remote, and an abandoned railway running parallel to the canal adds its own ghostly accompaniment to the proceedings. Further spirits may well be present at ADDERLEY LOCKS, where a privet hedge by the third chamber down betrays the site of a long ago demolished lock-keeper's cottage.

Market Drayton

Market Drayton is an ancient Shropshire market town which always gave the impression that it welcomed visitors without going out of its way to attract them. All this has changed with the 'discovery' that Drayton, as the locals tend to call it, is "The Home of Gingerbread" and the town council now intend to put themselves firmly on the tourist map. You sense, however, that such trivialities are not to every inhabitant's taste in a place which seems happier going about its day to day routine with a certain amount of dour provincial restraint. Stroll through Drayton on a Sunday morning, when little throngs of the faithful are filing in to the Nonconformist chapels, and you'll see what we mean. Actually, the town lets its hair down much more unselfconciously on Wednesdays when the 700 year old market fills the town with country bumpkins intent on a bargain and a good gossip. This gregarious gathering is Market Drayton's real heritage - along with its handsome half-timbered town houses which mostly date from the aftermath of a fire that swept the town in 1651 - and it is these attributes that the local powers-that-be should accentuate and promote. You have to go back to the first quarter of the 18th century to

find the town's most famous son, Robert Clive, who by all accounts couldn't wait to get away. He's best remembered here for scaling the tower of St Mary's and blackmailing local shopkeepers. Such youthful escapades were ideal preparation for a career in diplomacy and military leadership. He established British rule in the sub-continent and became known as 'Clive of India'.

Eating & Drinking

Drayton bristles with pubs and Marstons beer predominates. Nearest to the canal, however, is THE TALBOT, an Ansells house just east of bridge 62 where bar meals are usually available. Centre stage in the town itself is the CORBET ARMS, High Street, an old coaching inn which does coffees (with gingerbread!), lunches, teas and dinners. Tel: MD 2961. Marston's THE RAILWAY at

the northern end of Cheshire Street is also worth investigating.

Shopping

Wednesdays, and to a lesser extent, Saturdays are

continued on page 52

Swanley Locks, at the pastoral eastern end of the Llangollen Canal.

Paired bridges, paired locks.
This page; Chirk Aqueduct, Llangollen Canal.
Opposite: Whitby Locks, Ellesmere Port, Shropshire Union Canal.

Split levels at Tower Wharf, Chester, Shropshire Union Canal.

FIFTEEN LOCKS running through a cutting of larch and Scots pine take the canal across the Shropshire/Cheshire border. The locks are well maintained and a pleasure to operate and raise or lower the canal almost a hundred feet. Towards the foot of this flight - known to the old boatmen as the Audlem 'Thick' - you pass Audlem wharf, one of the prettiest ports of call on the Shropshire Union, with a former warehouse restored as a popular pub and the adjacent lofty mill converted into a superb craft shop.

North of the bottom lock, below which is a well preserved stable block, the canal, wide with concrete banking but deceptively shallow, bounds across the infant river Weaver on a high embankment. An equal leap in your imagination is required to credit that, during the last war, there were proposals to make the river navigable, joining it to the Shropshire Union at this point by a barge lift, and replacing the lock flights at Audlem, Adderley and Tyrley with similar machinery, so that 100 ton capacity barges could trade between Merseyside and the Midlands. The concept echoed a plan launched in 1888 for a ship canal capable of handling 300 ton craft between Birmingham and the Mersey via the Potteries. Pleasure boaters can be thankful that no such schemes materialised, but there are those of us who do believe that inland waterways, properly invested in, could have a role to play in the safe, and environmentally harmonious carriage of heavy goods.

Audlem

Sleepy Audlem rarely gets into the guidebooks. motorists mistake its compactness for a lack of character, and have driven through before they have time to fall for its appealing mix of redbrick and timber buildings gathering at the feet of the noble parish church of St James the Great. Local buses depart from what must be the prettiest 'bus shelter' in England, an old oak beamed, stone pillared market cross. Here the village teenagers gather to oggle the opposite sex, or the old men meet to remember when such matters were paramount to them.

Eating & Drinking

With two canalside pubs and three up in the village, Audlem is spoilt for choice. Current consensus favours THE LAMB (to the left of the market cross, beyond the chemist) both for its atmosphere and the standard of its cooking; Tetley bitter, draught Guinness. THE BRIDGE (canalside bridge 78) is an old boatman's pub, suitably refurbished, dispensing Marstons and offering a range of bar meals; children are catered for. THE SHROPPIE FLY is a former warehouse conversion overlooking lock 13. It serves Boddingtons and Stones bitters, bar and restaurant meals and children are welcome. The bar is formed from an old narrowboat.

Shopping

Friendly stores cater for most needs and make shopping here a pleasure rather than a time consuming chore. Lunchtime closing takes its toll, however, and half-day is Wednesday. Ice cream, made on the premises, is available from the confectioners by the market cross. The church advertises teas and coffees. Calor gas is sold by the garage adjacent to bridge 78. Audlem's outstanding establishment, though, is beside the canal itself. AUDLEM MILL CANAL SHOP was converted from the three-storey Kingbur Mill and has been fashioned into a splendid environment for the display of crafts and gifts; in fact, it is quite as charming as the gentleman who owns it, John Stothert.

Public Transport

BUSES – Cheshire Bus services to/from Nantwich (Mon-Sat) and Market Drayton (Weds only), both useful for towpath walkers. Tel: Crewe (0270) 505350 to check details.

AT HACK GREEN there are two isolated locks and the remnants of a stable, recalling the practice of frequent changes of horses on the 'fly' boats, which travelled day and night with urgent, perishable cargoes. This is the Cheshire Plain and dairy farming has long been a vital part of the area's economy. We tend to think of farming as an unchanging facet of the landscape, but the Fresian cattle so synonymous with the county are a relatively recent introduction. The working boatman of the 19th century would not recognise these black & white interlopers from the Low Countries. When he passed this way the pastures would have been grazed by indigenous breeds like Ayrshires and Alderneys.

The Birmingham & Liverpool Junction Canal was opened between Autherley and Nantwich in 1835 - the last major canal, other than the Manchester Ship Canal which was in a different league altogether, to be built in Britain. By the time it was opened, however, the canal promoters and builders had been overtaken by the Railway Age. Narrowboats carrying 25 tons at an average speed of 3mph were no competition for goods trains steaming along at 25mph trailing several hundred tons behind them. Nevertheless, after it was taken over by the London & North Western Railway in 1846, the Shropshire Union Canal continued to be well used, largely because it penetrated rival Great Western Railway territory, and there was a good deal of competition for cargoes.

In fact, commercial trade survived on this canal until the 1960s; which must be some sort of testimony to the viability of canal carrying. Perhaps in the final analysis attitudes rather than economics prevailed. One of the most celebrated traffics on the Shroppie in latter years was Thomas Clayton's oil run from Stanlow on the banks of the Mersey to Langley Green, near Oldbury in the Black Country. The contract commenced in 1924 and the Clayton boats, with their characteristic decked holds, and bearing the names of rivers, were a mainstay of trade on the canal for thirty years. Even post-war, a thousand boat-loads per annum were being dispatched from Stanlow, some remaining horse-drawn until the early Fifties. But, in common with other narrow canals, the Shropshire Union lost its final freights to the motor lorry. And, for many, with the disappearence of its working boats, something died on the Shroppie; some intangible component of canal heritage that no amount of preservation, nor hectic holiday trade, can compensate for.

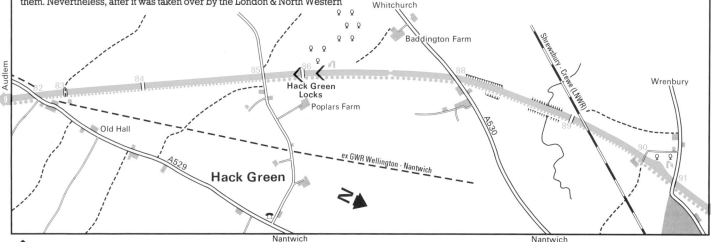

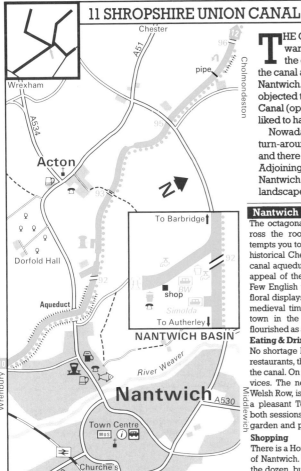

THE CHARACTER OF the Shropshire Union Canal changes perceptibly at Nantwich: northwards lie the broad, winding waters of its earlier constituent, the Chester Canal; southwards the direct and narrow Birmingham & Liverpool Junction Canal. A broad embankment elevates the canal above the housing, back gardens and allotments which constitute the periphery of Nantwich. Ironically, these earthworks could have been avoided if the owners of Dorfold Hall had not objected to the passage of the canal across their land. The basin and former terminus of the Chester Canal (opened in 1779) indicates the more expedient route to the south which Telford would have liked to have used.

Nowadays the basin is used by British Waterways own hire fleet and presents a busy scene on turn-around days. Other than at weekends, there are usually temporary moorings available here, and there is a certain pleasure to be had from manouevering in and out of its narrow confines. Adjoining the basin are the premises of the Nantwich & Border Counties Yachting Club. Between Nantwich and Hurleston Junction (Map 12) the old Chester Canal passes uneventfully through a landscape typical of the Cheshire Plain.

Nantwich

The octagonal tower of St Mary's church, glimpsed across the rooftops from the high canal embankment, tempts you to moor and get to know this picturesque and historical Cheshire town. Walking in from the basin, the canal aqueduct forms an appropriate portcullis, and the appeal of the town increases as the centre is reached. Few English towns are cleaner or better endowed with floral displays, and the centre is mercifully traffic free. In medieval times Nantwich was the chief salt producing town in the county. For a brief Victorian heyday it flourished as a spa town.

Eating & Drinking

No shortage here of tearooms, coaching inns and ethnic restaurants, though all are at least 15 minutes walk in from the canal. On this occasion we'll leave you to your own devices. The nearest pub, THE ODDFELLOWS ARMS on Welsh Row, is little over 5 minutes away, however, and it's a pleasant Tetley house offering home made cooking both sessions, daily. Children are welcome and there's a garden and playground at the rear of the pub.

Shopping

There is a Home Counties air of affluence about the shops of Nantwich. There are antique shops and boutiques by the dozen, but what is most satisfying is the sheer quality of the food sellers: butchers like Clewlows and bakers like Chatwins, both of whom have branches in Pepper Street. The market is held of Thursdays and Saturdays; Wednesday is half day. The marina shop stocks a selection of provisions, and there is also an excellent corner shop on the corner of the Wrenbury road, easily reached from the aqueduct if you're passing through.

Places to Visit

TOURIST INFORMATION CENTRE – Beam Street (by bus station). Tel: Nantwich (0270) 623914.

NANTWICH MUSEUM – Pillory Street. Open daily, 10.30am – 4.30pm (ex Wed & Sun). Interesting displays of local history; salt, chesse etc. Tel: Nantwich 627104.

Public Transport

BUSES – services from bus station to all parts of the region. Tel: Crewe (0270) 505350. Service C84 (Hanley-Chester) calls at Barbridge and Calveley, making it useful for towpath walkers.

TRAINS – bi-hourly service to/from Crewe and Shrewsbury Mon-Sat. Tel: Shrewsbury (0743) 64041.

Boatyards & Hire Bases

NANTWICH MARINA (British Waterways) – Chester Road, Nantwich, Cheshire CW5 8LB. Tel: Nantwich (0270) 625122. 4 to 8 berth hire craft, day boat. Pumpout, gas, drydock, shop with chandlery, gifts and groceries.

SIMOLDA – Basin End, Nantwich, Cheshire CW5 8LA. Tel: Nantwich (0270) 624075. 3 to 8 berth hire craft.

HURLESTON AND BARBRIDGE are the 'Clapham Junctions' of the inland waterways. During the cruising season the section between them is often frenetic with boats converging and diverging to and from all points of the canal compass. Fortunately the old Chester Canal was built to barge dimensions and there is plenty of room to manoeuvre. The Cheshire Plain's recurring image of spacious pastures grazed by Fresian cattle continues unabated. At milking time the herds shuffle with heavy udders across the occupation bridges of the canal. Remote and seemingly always windswept, the Middlewich Branch of the Shropshire Union cuts across the grain of the landscape on a series of high embankments. It can be a busy length of canal for, as well as Four Counties Ring traffic, it funnels boats to and from the popular . Llangollen Canal. Its four locks, which are deep and heavy gated, can become bottlenecks at the beginning and end of summer weeks.

Historically, the branch, opened in 1833, belonged to the Chester Canal Company and was engineered by Thomas Telford. Trade was heavy in cargo-carrying days too. In 1888 a curious experiment was undertaken to replace horse power by laying a narrow gauge railway along the towpath below Cholmondeston Lock and employing small steam locomotives to haul strings of narrowboats. The concept didn't develop here, though it did catch on abroad, especially on the French waterways.

Barbridge Junction

An incredibly popular overnight mooring spot – you need to get here early to be sure of a space. The main road apart, it is easy to see its attraction, with two canalside pubs vying for custom and the interest of the junction itself, where once a transhipment shed spanned the main line. You can detect its site where the canal narrows just to the south of the junction. Brian Collings did an evocative painting of it in Tom Foxon's working boatman's memoirs "Anderton for Orders".

Eating & Drinking

Heads or tails?: the BARBRIDGE INN (bridge 100) serves Boddingtons, the JOLLY TAR (opposite junction – watch the traffic!) does Greenalls; both cater well for families, offer the choice between bar and restaurant meals, and have nice big gardens.

Public Transport

BUSES - Crosville C84 hourly, daily to/from Chester and Hanley via Nantwich.

Shopping

Post office stores (off licence) open daily adjacent to Barbridge Junction. Also from Venetian Marine at Cholmondeston – see below.

Boatyards

BARBRIDGE MARINA – Wardle, Nantwich CW5 6BE. Tel: Wettenhall (027073) 682. Elsan disposal, gas, moorings, servicing & repairs, slipway, boatbuilding, sales & brokerage, chandlery, boat transport.
VENETIAN MARINE – Cholmondeston, Nantwich CW5 6DD. Tel: Wettenhall (027073) 251 & 381. Elsan disposal, water, gas, rubbish disposal, moorings, repairs & servicing, slipway, boat sales and chandlery. Provisions.

* Estimated time refers to main line - allow 1½hrs for this section of Middlewich Branch.

THIS is an intoxicating length of waterway full of contrasts in landscape: the wooded defile at Tilstone Bank; the glorious line of close-cropped hills running north of the two Beeston locks; and, most dramatic of all for travellers heading northwards, the first detailed glimpses of Beeston Castle, over five hundred feet high on its lonely outcrop. Through all this the little river Gowy chuckles to its Mersey outfall, draining the rolling farmland. But, scintillating scenery apart, it bears remembering that the old Chester Canal had a living to earn and throughout this section there are well preserved examples of former commerce. At Calveley there was a transhipment wharf between canal and railway. The Shropshire Union once thought seriously about converting the canal into a railway southwards from here to Wolverhampton. Such might-have-beens are the essence of history, but we must be relieved that this particular proposal never came to fruition.

Bunbury is a fascinating canal environment. The widebeam staircase locks make an obvious centrepiece. Alongside them is a fine stable block, recalling the practice of exchanging fresh horses for tired ones on the fast 'fly-boats', which covered the 80 miles between the Mersey ports and the Black Country factories in just over 24 hours. These premises are now used by Dartline for building and maintaining boats. Their offices and shop are accomodated in an adjacent warehouse still displaying the painted legend "SHROPSHIRE UNION RAILWAY & CANAL Co" on its north facing gable end. Tilstone Lock lies in a gorgeous setting. Beside it stands a former mill astride the Gowy, dating from 1838 and tenderly restored for residential use. A curious circular building stands at the head of the lock chamber.

There are others at Beeston Stone and Tarvin locks and they were once used by lengthsmen to keep maintenance equipment in. Beneath a sweeping ridge reminiscent of the South Downs, stand the two Beeston locks; the upper built conventionally of stone, the lower unusually of iron plates, being Thomas Telford's solution to conquer the instabillity of the ground below at this point.

Bunbury

The village itself lies a mile or so to the south along a minor road bordered by prosperous looking farms. The parish church is a notable structure. BUNBURY MILL, a restored water mill beside the Gowy, ½ mile south-west of bridge 105, is open to the public on summer weekend afternoons. Groceries are available from DARTLINE

Beeston

Beyond the railway from bridge 107 are auction rooms and a cattle market usually open on Wednesdays and Fridays. Visitors are free to wander among the pens and stalls, experiencing the authentic face of the countryside. The hills behind hide camouflaged oil dumps dating from World War II. At STONE LOCK COTTAGE Caroline and Ken Docherty run a delightful canalside outlet for delicious home baking, preserves, goats milk, cheese and locally made ice cream. The BEESTON CASTLE HOTEL – adjacent to bridge 107, is a Bass pub usually serving bar meals, families are catered for. Across the road is a newsagent with a small groceries section.

Boatyards & Hire Bases
DARTLINE – Canal Wharf, Bunbury, Tarporley, Ches. CW6 9QB. Tel: Bunbury (0829) 260638. 2 to 12 berth hire craft (Blakes). Day boats for hire. Pumpout, diesel, gas, moorings, repairs & servicing, slipway, boatbuilding, sales & brokerage, chandlery, shop with gifts, groceries, books, maps etc; payphone.
CHAS. HARDERN & CO – Beeston Castle Wharf, Beeston, Tarporley, Ches. CW6 9NH. Tel: Tarporley (0829) 732595. 2 to 6 berth hire craft. Pumpout, water, diesel, gas, rubbish disposal, repairs & servicing and particularly charming gift shop.

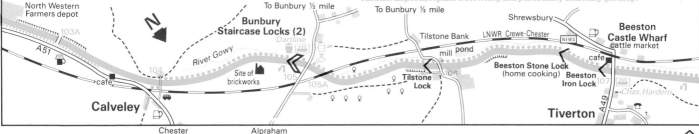

BEESTON Castle unmistakeably dominates the landscape, like a visitor from another planet, an upturned plum pudding of an outcrop, a geological afterthought commandeered by Medieval man for a fortress. Behind it the Peckforton Hills ride the horizon like surfers on an Atlantic beach. A million years ago Cheshire was a desert, which accounts for the redness of the soil to this day. The hills were created by earth movements fracturing the desert floor and pushing huge lumps of rock upwards. Compared to this, two centuries of the canal seem just a scratch on the veneer of time. This is good walking country. The Sandstone Trail, a 30 mile footpath across Cheshire's backbone from Overton to Whitchurch, crosses the canal at Wharton's Lock and can conveniently be linked with the towpath and other public footpaths to form a number of circular rambles.

The "Shady Oak" is a pleasant canalside inn which few travellers will resist visiting. Across the canal another Gowy mill survives as someone's enviable private residence. A country road swoops down to cross the millstream and an adjacent expanse of water is busy with wildfowl. Nearby, the canal is carried over the Gowy on an embankment framed with conifers. Trains thread their way through the fields in the middle distance, but otherwise the world seems undisturbed. In the long pound between Wharton's and Christleton locks the boater has plenty of time for peaceful reflection and communion with nature.

Map showing the canal route with Beeston Castle, Tattenhall, LNWR Crewe-Chester railway, River Gowy, Bate's Mill, Wharton's Lock, "Shady Oak", bridges 108-114, Aqueduct, "Aldersey Arms", To Tattenhall 1½ miles, Huxley, Brassey Green, To Tarporley 2 miles, Sandstone Trail. N compass.

Beeston Castle
Eating & Drinking
SHADY OAK – canalside bridge 109. Comfortable waterside pub popular with canal travellers, motorists and ramblers on the "Sandstone Trail". Imaginative menu. Children welcome in one room if eating. Pleasant garden with play area. Payphone.
ALDERSEY ARMS – near bridge 113. Good country pub offering a variety of beers, bar and restaurant meals. Children's playground. Payphone.

Places to Visit
BEESTON CASTLE – 1 mile south of canal along Sandstone Trail from Wharton's Lock, or by road from Bate's mill if you're shod by Gucci. Open daily but afternoons only on Sundays. Admission charge. Tel: Tattenhall (0829) 260464. Perched at the top of its sheer rock you would have expected this 13th century fortress to have deterred most beligerents. Yet it was captured at least three times during its turbulent history: first by Simon de Montfort in his revolt against Henry III; and then twice during the Civil War when first the Roundheads, then the Cavaliers, then the Roundheads again held it.

After the Wars of the Roses the castle was allowed to fall into decay, and after the Civil War the victorious Parliamentarians destroyed much of it. Legend has it that Richard the Lionheart buried treasure in the castle well, a rumour strong enough to warrant searches to be made in 1842 and 1935, but both were fruitless so the castle keeps its secret. The only deterrent todays visitor has to face is the climb. But the wonderful panorama which the view from the upper keep provides makes this well worthwhile. Canal travellers can pick out the course of the Shropshire Union all the way to Egg Bridge.

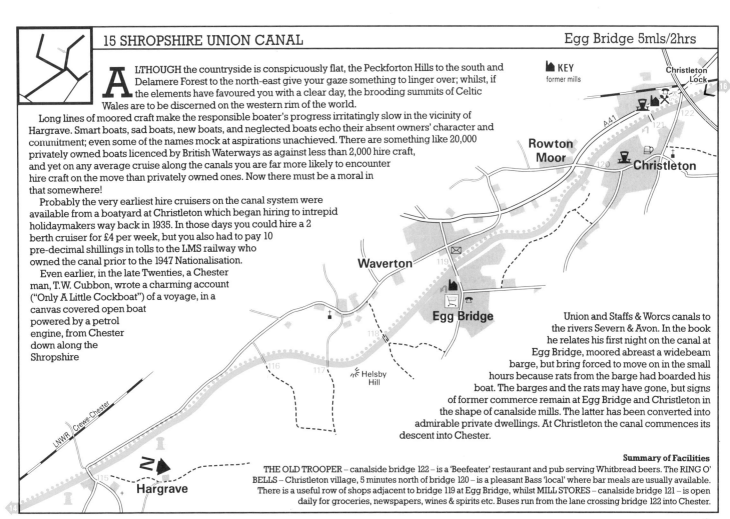

ALTHOUGH the countryside is conspicuously flat, the Peckforton Hills to the south and Delamere Forest to the north-east give your gaze something to linger over; whilst, if the elements have favoured you with a clear day, the brooding summits of Celtic Wales are to be discerned on the western rim of the world.

Long lines of moored craft make the responsible boater's progress irritatingly slow in the vicinity of Hargrave. Smart boats, sad boats, new boats, and neglected boats echo their absent owners' character and commitment; even some of the names mock at aspirations unachieved. There are something like 20,000 privately owned boats licenced by British Waterways as against less than 2,000 hire craft, and yet on any average cruise along the canals you are far more likely to encounter hire craft on the move than privately owned ones. Now there must be a moral in that somewhere!

Probably the very earliest hire cruisers on the canal system were available from a boatyard at Christleton which began hiring to intrepid holidaymakers way back in 1935. In those days you could hire a 2 berth cruiser for £4 per week, but you also had to pay 10 pre-decimal shillings in tolls to the LMS railway who owned the canal prior to the 1947 Nationalisation.

Even earlier, in the late Twenties, a Chester man, T.W. Cubbon, wrote a charming account ("Only A Little Cockboat") of a voyage, in a canvas covered open boat powered by a petrol engine, from Chester down along the Shropshire Union and Staffs & Worcs canals to the rivers Severn & Avon. In the book he relates his first night on the canal at Egg Bridge, moored abreast a widebeam barge, but bring forced to move on in the small hours because rats from the barge had boarded his boat. The barges and the rats may have gone, but signs of former commerce remain at Egg Bridge and Christleton in the shape of canalside mills. The latter has been converted into admirable private dwellings. At Christleton the canal commences its descent into Chester.

KEY
former mills

Summary of Facilities

THE OLD TROOPER – canalside bridge 122 – is a 'Beefeater' restaurant and pub serving Whitbread beers. The RING O' BELLS – Christleton village, 5 minutes north of bridge 120 – is a pleasant Bass 'local' where bar meals are usually available. There is a useful row of shops adjacent to bridge 119 at Egg Bridge, whilst MILL STORES – canalside bridge 121 – is open daily for groceries, newspapers, wines & spirits etc. Buses run from the lane crossing bridge 122 into Chester.

THE canal traveller's approach to Chester is overtly suburban and industrial, characteristics which belie the grace and romance of the city within its walls. Frankly, you could be forgiven thinking that a Burnley or a Blackburn lay immediately ahead and it is with some relief that the centre is reached and the Chester of the guidebooks manifests itself. The expected climax shouldn't be rushed though, workaday Chester has its highlights: the dour Victorian waterworks below Chemistry Lock, and then the high lead shot tower and gaunt warehouses which overlook the canal as it passes through an area of the city once commercially paramount to the coffers of the Shropshire Union. Wide beam barges known as Mersey 'flats' traded down from Ellesmere Port to Chester and, less commonly, southwards to Barbridge and Nantwich. North of the city centre lies Tower Wharf and the short Dee Branch linking the canal with the river. The canalscape here is terrific, comprising of Telford's warehouse with its arched loading bay; an elegant canopied drydock; a massive boatbuilding yard where the Shropshire Union carrying fleet was once built and maintained, and the rare fascination of two adjacent canal levels.

But it is the canal's juxtaposition with Chester's great red medieval wall which is its most memorable gesture and image. The round tower from which King Charles I saw his Cavaliers beaten looms out over the water so dramatically that the canal resembles a defensive moat, which is exactly what it once was, and the canal builders took good advantage of this fortunate channel, presumably discovering, though we could find no written account, a certain amount of Roman remains in the process. Not so easy, was the construction of the gargantuan Northgate staircase locks which had to be hewn out of solid rock. They raise the canal over thirty feet

and are memorable for the steerer and lock worker alike: the former experiencing a shadowy immersion in the gloomy depth of each successive chamber; the latter the frustration of the slow equation of levels compounded by the provision of single paddles. Tempers are apt to fray at this point. Calm yourself by regarding the serene facade of Harvest House, formerly the headquarters of the Shropshire Union Company, which overlooks the railway bridge in an epitomy of Georgian dignity. Equally dignified, is the regular passage between Tower Wharf and Cow Lane of a horse drawn passenger boat, a charming procession from the past and a happy way for the visitor, careless enough to come by means other than boat, to see the wall from water level.

The Chester Canal predated the Wirral Line by a matter of twenty years or so and, originally, the link with the river Dee continued direct from the foot of Northgate locks, which at that time consisted of five chambers. The existing layout dates from the advent of the route from Ellesmere Port and the branch down to the Dee describes a dogleg course through three locks to meet the tidal river. To all intents and purposes it is 'out of bounds' to hire craft, though private owners may use the branch for mooring or reaching the river if due notice is given to the relevant officials. Downstream of Chester the river flows fast and is not a navigation to be taken lightly. Upstream the fourteen meandering miles to Farndon are more placid but a weir must be negotiated at high tide and a licence obtained from the council. Quite the easiest way to enjoy the Dee is to hire a rowing boat at The Groves or catch one of Bithells launches which operate sightseeing cruises of varying duration.

Chester

On Sunday mornings Chester breathes like a sleeping child and footsteps softly echo your progress around the city wall, the perfect introduction to this loveliest of cities. At most other times, though, shoppers and sight-seers transform Chester into a frenetic, free-for-all from which you are apt to go scurrying back to your boat for refuge. But in all of Britain's 2,000 navigable miles of inland waterway, only York can vie with Chester when it comes to antiquity, and the city wall, which kept enemies at bay down the centuries, now keeps 20th century reality in its place. Once through the ancient gateways, you are wrapped in a Medieval time warp which makes Chester

the most agreeable of places to saunter in; crowds permitting. It was the Romans who founded the city, seeing it as a likely place to build a port and keep a weather eye upon the troublesome Marches; they called it Deva. In the Dark Ages the Anglo-Saxons undid much of their predecessors civilisation, but by the Middle Ages Chester was flourishing again and a 12th century writer noted ships from Aquitane, Germany and Spain at berth in the shadow of the city wall. Chester's celebrated 'Rows' are thought to have had their origins during this period. These covered galleries above street level are quite unique, and turn window-shopping into a particular pleasure. During the Civil War the city supported King

Charles, but it did him little good, for it was from the walls of Chester that he saw his army defeated on Rowton Heath. Victorian Chester grew up outside the city wall, beyond the canal and out towards the railway. What the Victorians did inside the wall is best forgotten by those romantics who like to think that all that black & white half timbering is original. Today, though, Chester knows that it pays to look old. People come from all over the world to walk the walls and to find a kind of hush in the dignified Cathedral. Those who make there way here by water stand to gain the most of all.

continued on page 26

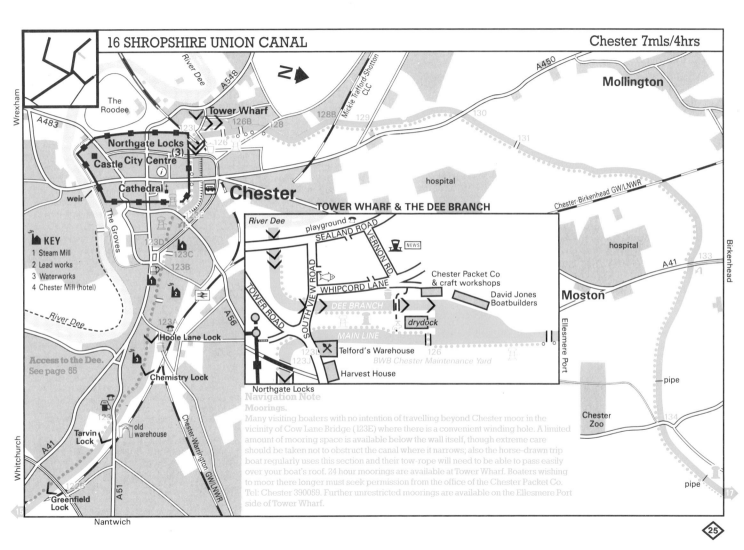

Wrexham

A483

The Roodee

River Dee

A548

N

Mickle Trafford-Shotton CLC

A450

Mollington

Tower Wharf

126B

128

128B

129

130

131

hospital

Chester-Birkenhead GW/LNWR

123B

126

Northgate Locks (3)

Castle **City Center**

i

Cathedral

Chester

weir

TOWER WHARF & THE DEE BRANCH

hospital

A41

133

Birkenhead

The Groves

KEY
1 Steam Mill
2 Lead works
3 Waterworks
4 Chester Mill (hotel)

123D

123C

123B

1

2

River Dee

River Dee

playground

SEALAND ROAD

VERNON RD.

NEWS

SOUTH VIEW ROAD

Chester Packet Co & craft workshops

David Jones Boatbuilders

Moston

A56

123A

DEE BRANCH

WHIPCORD LANE

TOWER ROAD

drydock

Ellesmere Port

Hoole Lane Lock

MAIN LINE

Access to the Dee.
See page 55

3

126

Telford's Warehouse

BWB Chester Maintenance Yard

123

123

pipe

Chemistry Lock

Harvest House

Northgate Locks

Chester Zoo

134

old warehouse

Tarvin Lock

A41

Whitchurch

Chester-Warrington GW/LNWR

A51

122B

Greenfield Lock

Nantwich

pipe

Navigation Note
Moorings.
Many visiting boaters with no intention of travelling beyond Chester moor in the vicinity of Cow Lane Bridge (123E) where there is a convenient winding hole. A limited amount of mooring space is available below the wall itself, though extreme care should be taken not to obstruct the canal where it narrows; also the horse-drawn trip boat regularly uses this section and their tow-rope will need to be able to pass easily over your boat's roof. 24 hour moorings are available at Tower Wharf. Boaters wishing to moor there longer must seek permission from the office of the Chester Packet Co. Tel: Chester 390059. Further unrestricted moorings are available on the Ellesmere Port side of Tower Wharf.

continued from page 24

Eating & Drinking

No shortage here of establishments to suit all tastes and credit card balances, so the following is, by definition, a personal and intuitive selection: PARIS BRIOCHE, Bridge Street Row, a continental style all day cafe/restaurant where the croissants and cafetiere are just the thing to put pep into flagging tourists. Two canalside warehouses conversions are: OLD HARKERS by bridge 123B and TELFORD'S WAREHOUSE at Tower Wharf. For a traditional pub try the ODDFELLOW'S ARMS adjacent bridge 123E; bar lunches and Greenall beers. More sophisticated, and correspondingly expensive, are THE BLUE BELL, Northgate and CLAVERTONS, Lower Bridge Street. Relatively inexpensive grills for hungry boating families are catered for by the CRITERION BERNI INN on Eastgate Row and the WITCHES KITCHEN, Frodsham Street (adjacent bridge 123E).

Shopping

One of the best, most civilised shopping centres in England. Look out for: THE ROWS – some of the city's most upmarket shops go about their business above street level in these fascinating galleries. ST MICHAEL'S ARCADE – A splendid Victorian arcade of soaring iron and glass reached off Bridge Street Row. GROSVENOR PRECINCT – discreet modern development tucked unobtrusively between Eastgate and Bridge Street. THE FORUM – indoor market open daily ex Wed pm and Sun. Thriving stalls specialise in fresh Cheshire produce, crafts and antiques.

Places to Visit

CHESTER CATHEDRAL – One of England's ecclesiastical masterworks. Splendid red sandstone exterior, enthralling interior. Refreshments available in refectory.
CHESTER HERITAGE CENTRE – Bridge Street Row. Audio-visual portrayal of the city's history housed in a former church. Admission charge, open daily ex Wed. Tel: Chester 317948.
CHESTER VISITOR CENTRE – Vicar's Lane. Life-size reconstruction of a typical Chester street in Victorian times replete with sounds and smells. Admission charge, open daily. Tel: Chester 318916.

GROSVENOR MUSEUM – Grosvenor Street. City museum of local history. Open Mon-Sat and Sun pm. Admission free. Tel: Chester 321616
TOURIST INFORMATION CENTRE – Town Hall, Northgate. Open daily. Tel: Chester (0244) 318356.
BOAT TRIPS – On the river Dee from the boating Station at The Groves. Cruises aboard Bithells launches of varying duration or self-steer craft for hire by hour or day. Tel: Chester 325394 On the canal from Tower Wharf by horse-drawn narrowboat operated by the Chester Packet Co. Tel: Chester 390059.
CHESTER ZOO – Caughall Road, Chester. Tel: Chester (0244) 380280. Open daily admission charge. Most easily reached from canal by way of bridge 134. One of Europe's largest zoos where they try hard to exhibit the animals in their natural habitat. Also features many acres of landscaped grounds which incorporate a mini-system of waterways on which you can ride by waterbus.
SIGHTSEEING WALKS – Accompanied walks depart from the Tourist Information Centre. Several themes are available including 'Roman Soldier Wall Patrol' and 'Ghost Hunter Trail'. Further details from Publicity Department, City Council, Town Hall. Tel: Chester 324324

Public Transport

BUSES – bus station on George Street off Northgate. Tel: Chester (0244) 602666.
TRAINS – railway station on City Road reached via bridge 123B. Useful half-hourly service (hourly Sundays) to Ellesmere Port if you haven't time to reach the Boat Museum by water. Tel: Chester (0244) 340170.

Boatyards

DAVID JONES – Cambrian View, Chester, CH1 4DE. Tel: Chester (0244) 376363. Traditional boatyard based in premises once belonging to the Shropshire Union company. Emphasis on repair & servicing of historic craft and larger vessels.

COMPARITIVELY few boaters, reaching Chester from the south, elect to continue along the Shropshire Union main line to its historic terminus on the banks of the river Mersey at Ellesmere Port. Beguiled by Chester's magnificence they languish in its spell, prisoners of the misconception that nothing worthy of their attention lies beyond Tower Wharf. In fact, exploring the northern end of the Shropshire Union and stopping short at Chester is akin to not listening to the end of Beethoven's 5th Symphony, or electing not to see the cheese board at the Savoy. Travelling northwards, urban Chester is soon left astern and one enters seemingly remote pastureland of no great beauty, but where peace prevails. More linear moorings slow the boater, but such delays can be redeemed as you near Ellesmere Port where a good depth of water enables the throttle to be exercised without fear of making a wash.

Dating from 1795, the canal between Chester and Ellesmere Port was part of the grandiose Ellesmere Canal scheme to link the Mersey with the Severn. Known as the Wirral line, it quickly attracted traffic; not only freight but passenger too, for a horse-drawn packet service connected Chester with Ellesmere Port where travellers could change to another boat to reach Liverpool. The passenger business flourished until the coming of the Railway Age, freight well into it. Indeed narrowboats continued to trade from Ellesmere Port with oil for the Midlands until the mid 1950s. One of the most famous of these craft, *Gifford* can be seen at the Boat Museum. Now, of course, the railway too has declined; hard to believe that boat trains once raced this way from London to connect with Atlantic liners on the Mersey. Today's more mundane transport makes an appearance at Stoak in the shape of two motorways.

Northwards from Stoak, the gleaming refineries of Stanlow define themselves on the horizon, indicating that Ellesmere Port is near at hand. No-one would pretend, even in a guidebook, that the approach to the town

continued on page 28

THE BOAT MUSEUM

Town Centre

Island Warehouse

housing

Lower Basin

Swingbridge

Lighthouse

P

Ticket Office

hotel

SHIP CANAL

Wervin

16

Top Farm

135

11

15

M56

Stoak

136

"Bunbury Arms"

137

138

139

140

140A

141

A5117

M53

142

Helsby Hill

Stanlow Refineries

144

stadium

gasometers

145

146

Ellesmere Port

A5032

Boat Museum

MUS

container dock

Manchester Ship Canal

The Mersey & Liverpool

Eastham

Manchester

is pretty, but anticipation outweighs purely aesthetic considerations, and you sense a rising excitement waiting for your first sight of the Mersey. Fortunately there is no anti-climax. Over two miles wide at this point, the river lies before you like the sea itself. On the horizon the northern bank of the Mersey can be traced from the old lighthouse at Hale, up past Speke airport, to a Liverpool made obvious by the twin towers of the two cathedrals. In the middle distance marshland oozes into mudbank. In the foreground vessels glide along the ship canal on their way to or from the high seas.

A limited amount of mooring space is usually available adjacent to bridge 147 for boaters intending to stay for just a short time in the vicinity. Preferable in our opinion, though, are the spacious moorings in the lower basin reached through the locks. Here you can lie beside some of the Boat Museum's larger exhibits. Whilst our research crew were there the preserved ICI 'Brunner' barge *Cuddington* came and berthed alongside on its way back from a waterway festival at Birkenhead. Nothing could have been more calculated to crystalise the latent atmosphere of the Port. As dusk fell Telford's little lighthouse stood silhouetted against the twinkling lights of Liverpool. The old barges strained at their mooring ropes and the spirits of the lost seamen and stevedores became almost tangible in the darkness.

Ellesmere Port, the 'port' of the Ellesmere Canal, dates from the last decade of the 18th century. The Wirral Line of the Ellesmere Canal met the Mersey here at what had, until then, been simply the small village of Netherpool. The opening of the Birmingham & Liverpool Junction Canal and later the Manchester Ship Canal turned these docks into a transhipment complex of almost unique significance. Happily, surviving official neglect typical of the 1960s, much of the infrastructure has been saved and incorporated into The Boat Museum, one of the country's premier collections of preserved inland waterway craft. One can't help but mourn, however, the loss through fire damage in 1970, just as the notion of the museum was beginning to take shape, of Telford's superb 'Winged Warehouses', three blocks of four storey structures which spanned part of the lower basin. Aerial photographs and diagrams reproduced in the museum's excellent guide book illustrate the extent of the port past and present and emphasise the debt of gratitude we owe to the small band of enthusiasts who began the collection of preserved craft which forms the basis of the museum.

Navigation Note
Under normal conditions, pleasure craft are denied access from the Lower Basin at Ellesmere Port to the Manchester Ship Canal. However, pleasure craft may navigate the MSC by arrangement if they comply with certain preconditions and pay an appropriate toll. See page 55 for further details.

Ellesmere Port

Ellesmere Port is a town with the sea in its blood if not on its doorstep. Snatches of conversation overhead in pubs and shops pertain to ships and seafarers and there's a salty, effervescent tang to the air which makes you long to weigh anchor and take to the high seas. Regrettably, though, nowadays Ellesmere Port seems to attach more importance to the manufacture of cars than to its traditional activities of stevedoring and wharfingering, and one senses that the emphasis has moved away from the seaward end of the town.

Eating & Drinking
GROSVENOR HOTEL – Upper Mersey Street (adjacent Boat Museum). Sprawling, atmospheric pub which makes few concessions to tourism but evokes instead an authentic feel of the docklands. Tetley-Walker, bar lunches, children catered for.

Shopping
All services in the town centre 10 minutes walk from the canal through the graffiti-covered underpass. Good indoor retail market and surprisingly large modern precinct featuring all the usual names.

Places to Visit
THE BOAT MUSEUM – Dockyard Road, Ellesmere Port, South Wirral L65 4EF. Tel: 051-355 5017. Open daily except winter Fridays. **Admission charge, but users of this guidebook can obtain a '2 for the price of 1' entry by showing a copy on arrival.**
Excellent museum housing Britain's most extensive collection of preserved inland waterway working craft. The old port makes an ideal setting for these boats and barges and many of the former warehouses and ancillary buildings have been restored as display areas illustrating the growth of the canal system. Boat trips are operated

along the Shropshire Union, refreshments are available and there's a well stocked souvenir shop with a wide selection of canal literature on sale. Special events, such as the popular 'Easter Boaters' Gathering' of traditional craft, are held throughout the year, contact the museum for further details.

Public Transport
BUSES – Frequent services to Chester, Birkenhead etc from bus station situated in town centre. Tel: Chester (0244) 602666.
TRAINS – Useful half-hourly frequency (hourly on Sundays) service to Hooton (for Liverpool) and Chester. Tel: 051-709 9696.

18 LLANGOLLEN CANAL

ALL summer long, painted narrow boats glide through the broad emerald pastures of the Cheshire Plain, as measuredly as the high Cumulus clouds in the wide Cheshire skies above. At Hurleston Junction a good proportion of them leave the main line of the old Shropshire Union, climb the four locks beside the reservoir embankment, and set off on the voyage to Wales. In terms of popularity 'The Llangollen' is the Blackpool of the canal system, but it has none of that seaside resort's vulgarity and it owes its heavy holiday traffic to the enduring charm of its scenery and the vivid drama of its destination.

Hurleston locks raise the canal 34 feet. The reservoir stores water, that has flowed down the canal from the river Dee at Horseshoe Falls above Llangollen itself, before it is treated and piped to the kitchen sinks of Crewe. Thank your lucky stars for this water, without it the LMS railway would have closed the canal during the second world war, because trade had long since ceased. In fact, technically the canal was 'abandoned', and it was only its use as a water channel that saved it from the dereliction suffered by other LMS owned canals under the infamous Act of 1944. Slowy a new traffic of pleasure boats began using the canal, forcing a passage through the weedy channel and decaying lock chambers. Under the 1968 Transport Act the Llangollen Canal (as the section of the old Ellesmere Canal between Hurleston and Llangollen had become known) was classified as a 'cruiseway', its position as one of the premier canal holiday routes assured for posterity. Each year over four thousand boat crews explore the canal, making it a vital component of the tourist economy of the region. Ironically, as we shall see further up the canal, the promoters of the canal never had this route in mind at all.

Between Hurleston and Wrenbury the Llangollen runs, somewhat surprisingly on a North-South axis; subconsciously one expects to be travelling East-West. Like walking through a field, nothing dramatic happens, but you feel good to be alive. The bucolic character of the surrounding countryside begins to influence your mood and you descend into rustic reverie. There are a pair of locks at Swanley and a trio at Baddiley (Map 19), the latter especially being something of a bottleneck at busy times, like Friday afternoon, when the exodus from Wales is at its height. Patience, patience!

Navigational Note

The flow of water down the Llangollen Canal tends to increase the running of the by-washes, causing a gush of water to run across the canal at the foot of locks. This can give the unwary a rough ride as they approach the lock chamber from below but collisions can be minimised by steering slightly into the overflow. Going downhill avoid being drawn over to the cill of the by-weir.

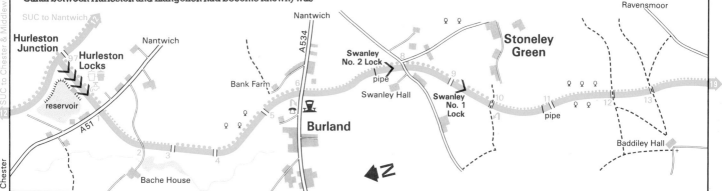

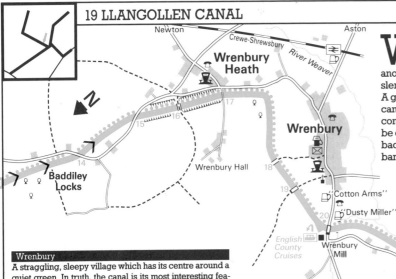

WRENBURY is one of the most picturesque ports of call at the English end of the Llangollen Canal. Lift bridge No.20 carries a country road across the canal by the village wharf, and another by-road parallels the waterway, separated from it only by a slender rail fence which somehow is suggestive of the Low Countries. A gushing headwater of the river Weaver is culverted beneath the canal and two former mill buildings, used now as a pub and a boatyard, complete what amounts to a particularly attractive scene crying out to be captured on canvas or film. The older of the two mill buildings dates back to the 16th century and is now "The Dusty Miller". On the opposite bank, the more modern mill appears to be of this century, being constructed in a handsome combination of grey corrugated iron and mellow orange coloured brick. The miller Arthur Sumner once operated a small fleet of narrowboats, but nowadays the mill is the base for a hire fleet and also houses a well stocked canal craft shop.

Wrenbury

A straggling, sleepy village which has its centre around a quiet green. In truth, the canal is its most interesting feature, and it is the wharf with its mellow old mills which attracts most visitors. At the far end of the village, beyond the infant Weaver, lies the railway station. Uncharacteristically, Beeching must have overlooked its existence, for it continues to be served by local trains on the Crewe – Shrewsbury line, offering towpath walkers the chance of one-way walks between Nantwich, Wrenbury and Whitchurch.

Eating & Drinking

COTTON ARMS – adjacent bridge 20. Greenalls ales, bar and restaurant meals, families welcomed, nice big garden with childrens adventure area. Good 'feedback' from CC users!

DUSTY MILLER – canalside bridge 20. Robinson's, bar & restaurant meals (book for latter on Nantwich 780537); canalside rose garden. A comfortable pub housed in a converted mill, pleasant restful ambience and freshly cooked food.

Shopping

Post office and general stores 5 minutes walk from the canal. There is also a useful store and newsagency at Wrenbury Heath near bridge 17.

Public Transport

TRAINS – station 1 mile east of bridge 20. Mon-Sat service. Tel: Shrewsbury (0743) 64041.

Boatyard & Hire Base

ENGLISH COUNTY CRUISES – Wrenbury Mill, Wrenbury, Nantwich, Cheshire CW5 8HG. Tel: Nantwich (0270) 780544. 4 to 9 berth hire craft (Blue Riband Club). Pump-out (ex Fri & Sat), Elsan disposal, water, diesel, rubbish disposal, gas, moorings, repairs & servicing, crane/lift-out, showers, toilets and gift shop.

Marbury

Refer to page 32.

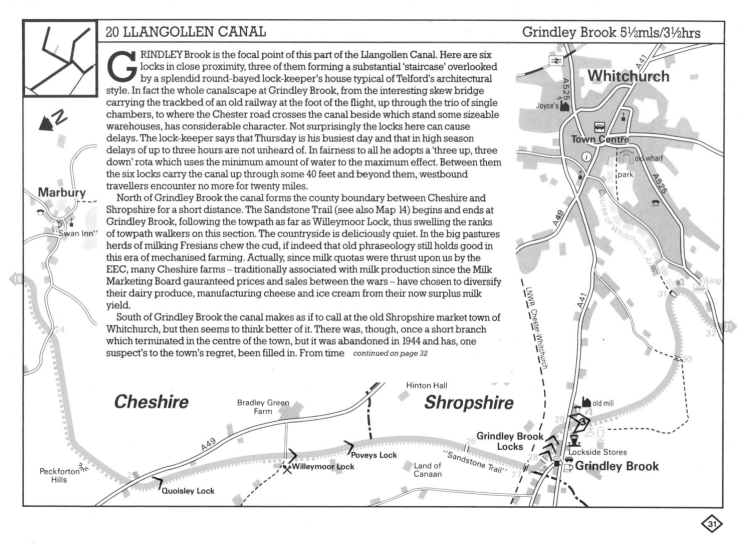

GRINDLEY Brook is the focal point of this part of the Llangollen Canal. Here are six locks in close proximity, three of them forming a substantial 'staircase' overlooked by a splendid round-bayed lock-keeper's house typical of Telford's architectural style. In fact the whole canalscape at Grindley Brook, from the interesting skew bridge carrying the trackbed of an old railway at the foot of the flight, up through the trio of single chambers, to where the Chester road crosses the canal beside which stand some sizeable warehouses, has considerable character. Not surprisingly the locks here can cause delays. The lock-keeper says that Thursday is his busiest day and that in high season delays of up to three hours are not unheard of. In fairness to all he adopts a 'three up, three down' rota which uses the minimum amount of water to the maximum effect. Between them the six locks carry the canal up through some 40 feet and beyond them, westbound travellers encounter no more for twenty miles.

North of Grindley Brook the canal forms the county boundary between Cheshire and Shropshire for a short distance. The Sandstone Trail (see also Map 14) begins and ends at Grindley Brook, following the towpath as far as Willeymoor Lock, thus swelling the ranks of towpath walkers on this section. The countryside is deliciously quiet. In the big pastures herds of milking Fresians chew the cud, if indeed that old phraseology still holds good in this era of mechanised farming. Actually, since milk quotas were thrust upon us by the EEC, many Cheshire farms – traditionally associated with milk production since the Milk Marketing Board gauranteed prices and sales between the wars – have chosen to diversify their dairy produce, manufacturing cheese and ice cream from their now surplus milk yield.

South of Grindley Brook the canal makes as if to call at the old Shropshire market town of Whitchurch, but then seems to think better of it. There was, though, once a short branch which terminated in the centre of the town, but it was abandoned in 1944 and has, one suspect's to the town's regret, been filled in. From time continued on page 32 to time some local initiative or other recommends restoration of the arm, but a certain amount of building has taken place on the old bed of the canal and its restoration would be no easy task. Nevertheless part of its course makes an interesting approach to the town from bridge 31, and the terminus itself is readily apparent at the far end of Jubilee Park. One unusual cargo regularly carried from Whitchurch Wharf was cheese. Once a week a special boat departed on a two day run to Manchester, its hold covered by white canvas to defract the sun's rays.

Marbury

One of those 'quietest places under the sun' we all dream of escaping to one day. The church lych gate celebrates "Ye who live mid English pastures green". The tiny green has one of those circular seats around the trunk of a tree which cry out to be sat upon and lingered over. Below the village are two meres. A footpath leads down to the larger and you can watch the antics of the resident wildfowl from its reedy banks. Alternatively there's a secluded seat in the churchyard overlooking the Big Mere.

Eating & Drinking
THE SWAN INN – village centre, 5 minutes walk from bridges 23 or 24. Lovely country pub, Greenall's ales and imaginative menu.
WILLEY MOOR LOCK RESTAURANT – canalside at Willeymoor Lock. Free house and restaurant open lunchtimes and evenings throughout boating season.

Grindley Brook

Shopping
Having done their fair share of canal cruising, John and Mavis Hards are well attuned to the likely requirements of passing boaters and run the LOCKSIDE STORES appropriately, opening early and closing late, daily, throughout the season. Home made cooking, fresh dairy produce, and a good selection of groceries, toiletries, wines, ciders and beers share shelf space with locally produced craft and canalia.

Public Transport
BUSES – Mon-Sat service Chester – Whitchurch, approximately hourly. Tel: 03450 56785.

Grindley Brook.

Whitchurch

Cheese and clocks are Whitchurch's gifts to civilisation. Blue Cheshire cheese is characterised by a marbled effect and is one of the great, tangy blue cheeses in the world, so don't leave town without trying some. Joyce's, whose attractive factory is on Station Road, have been manufacturing clocks for eight generations. The tower clock of the prominent parish church is their's and dates from 1849. Whitchurch clocks have been exported all over the world and can be found on many railway stations and other public buildings. For a town, though, that derives some prosperity from clock making, Whitchurch seems a timeless sort of place, and one immune to the ebb and flow of fashion.

Eating & Drinking
OLD TOWN HALL VAULTS – St Mary's Street. A cosy Marston's pub which was the birthplace of Sir Edward German the composer of "Merrie England" and other light operatic works. Bar meals usually available.
YE OLDE SHOPPE – High Street. Unselfconsciously 'quaint' cafe providing inexpensive coffees, lunches and teas.

Shopping
All services can be found in the town centre 1 mile east of the canal. Early closing renders the place like a ghost town on Wednesday afternoons but it hooches on Fridays when the market is held. In common with most towns in this part of the world the bakers and butchers are especially good.

Places to Visit
TOURIST INFORMATION CENTRE – Civic Centre. High Street. Tel: Whitchurch (0948) 4577.

Boatyard & Hire Base
VIKING AFLOAT – head office at: Lowesmoor Wharf, Worcester WR1 2RX. Tel: Worcester (0905) 28667. Whitchurch base telephone: Whitchurch (0948) 2012. 2 to 8 berth hire craft. Pumpout, diesel, water, repairs & servicing. Well stocked shop with gifts, guides and groceries. Payphone.

SEEMINGLY all alone in the world, the canal crosses remote farmland parallel to the border between Shropshire and the detached part of Clwyd once known as Flintshire. There are no shops for miles and only one pub anywhere near the canal which is at Platt Lane. With no locks to operate the boater is thankful that the occasional lift bridge occupies his attention. Some of these structures are of wood construction, others of steel. The latter are gradually replacing the former as the wear and tear of passing boats and increasingly heavy road traffic takes its toll. The new bridges are also safer to operate, having hydraulically assisted mechanisms as opposed to the simple, and not always reliable, balance weights of the original bridges. Bridge 42 was actually demolished by an errant vehicle and the road closed for a year before a replacement in steel was erected.

Bridge 39 carries the decaying trackbed of the once proud Cambrian Railway's Oswestry, Ellesmere & Whitchurch line. Opened in 1863, the route just saw out its centenary before succumbing to the Beeching Axe. At the railway grouping of 1923 the line fell under Great Western Railway control and, in the summertime at least, was well used by excursionists heading for the sandy shorelines of the mid Wales coast. Now the old embankment earthworks run like a scar across the empty countryside and sapplings occupy the faded course of the permanent way. Just be grateful that the canal was not allowed to perish in the same callous fashion. The ingenuity of the British character is only matched by its perverse readiness to undo the great works it has done.

The Llangollen Canal crosses a strangely melancholy region of untenable peat mosses where green grazing gives way to mongrel blacks and browns, with the trunks of silver birch etched against the darker masses. Farming here is impossible. Instead the peat is cut commercially for horticultural use. Rare birds such as Snipe make this unvisited land their home. Dogs bark at the passing traveller from lonely smallholdings, some of which date from the 18th century Enclosures, when many displaced peasant farmers found sanctuary and a new life on the mosses. In their own quixotic way the mosses impinge themselves upon your consciousness more permanently than much of the more obviously attractive scenery to be found along the Llangollen Canal.

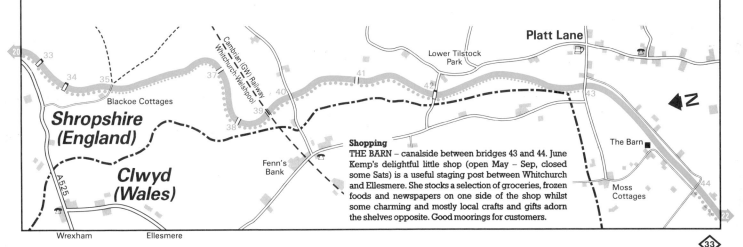

Shopping
THE BARN – canalside between bridges 43 and 44. June Kemp's delightful little shop (open May – Sep, closed some Sats) is a useful staging post between Whitchurch and Ellesmere. She stocks a selection of groceries, frozen foods and newspapers on one side of the shop whilst some charming and mostly local crafts and gifts adorn the shelves opposite. Good moorings for customers.

THERE is always something of a fascinating 'come hither' element about waterway junctions. However committed you are to the main line, a branch never fails to tempt you, seeming to dare you to explore whatever langorous charms lie just out of sight. At Whixall the old Prees Branch is no exception, and the remaining mile of what was once a four mile route makes a satisfying diversion from the main canal, often used by discerning boaters for quiet overnight moorings. Historically the branch was supposed to reach Prees but fell short of its objective by about a couple of miles. The actual terminus was established at Quina Brook. Here a bank of lime burning kilns were erected, for burnt lime was an important farming commodity in the innocent days before chemical fertilizers appeared on the scene. The mile of the Prees Branch which remains serves a boatyard built on the site of a puddle clay pit from which canal maintenance men extracted clay to line the canal bed. Beyond the boatyard its course is now a nature reserve. Two handsome wooden lift bridges survive on the arm. An unusual three-storey canal house watches over Prees Junction, its ground floor lying below the level of the embanked waterway.

Between Whixall Moss and Cadney Bank the canal passes through a somewhat claustrophobic corridor of dense woodland. For a brief interlude, between here and Hampton Bank, the canal finds itself in Wales. Hampton Bank is one of the Llangollen Canal's lesser sung engineering achievements. It carries the canal perhaps thirty feet above a headwater of the river Roden, a tributary of the Tern which joins the Severn below Shrewsbury. Tall larches mask the bank from the north wind. To the south-east beyond Wem stands Grinshill; to the north-west the mountains of Wales. Hampton was another place where lime burning for agriculture took place. L.T.C. Rolt moored here aboard *Cressy* for a month in the summer of 1947, having been thwarted in an attempt to reach Pontcysyllte because of excessive weed and general decay in the canal beyond Ellesmere.

Boatyards & Hire Bases
WHIXALL MARINA – Alders Lane, Whixall, Whitchurch, Shropshire SY13 2QP. Tel: Whixall (094872) 420. Pumpout, water, diesel, gas, repairs & servicing, long term secure moorings, drydock, slipway, shower and toilet block, brokerage, chandlery, gifts and provisions.

BLACK PRINCE HOLIDAYS – hire fleet based at Whixall but enquiries to: Stoke Prior, Bromsgrove, Worcs B60 4LA. Tel: Bromsgrove (0527) 575115.
BETTISFIELD PLEASURE BOATS – Canal Side, Bettisfield, Ellesmere, Shropshire. Tel: Bettisfield (094875) 465. 4 and 6 berth hire craft.

Lyneal Wharf

Course of Prees Branch to Quina Brook (Nature Reserve)

Whixall Marina

Black Prince

Shropshire (England)

Prees Junction

Cadney Moss

Clwyd (Wales)

Hampton Bank

Balmer Heath

B5063

Grinshill

Welsh Hills

Bettisfield

Whixall Moss

Shropshire (England)

Bettisfield Boats

N

Welshampton

THE old Shropshire market town of Ellesmere welcomes its eponymous canal. Yes, it's worth recalling that we know glibly today as the Llangollen Canal is a term which would be unfamiliar to the canal's promoters. For historically this was the Ellesmere Canal, an ambitious attempt to link the rivers Mersey, Dee and Severn with a main line from Chester to Shrewsbury. In the event, only the Pontcysyllte – Weston Lullingfields section was ever built with, from Welsh Frankton (see Map 24), branches to Llanymynech and Ellesmere itself. As it became apparent that the intended main line of the canal would never reach the Dee or the Severn, the Ellesmere Canal Company sought to link themselves to the rest of the inland waterway system by cutting a canal eastwards from Ellesmere to meet the Chester Canal near Nantwich. Hurleston was reached in 1805. Forty years later the Ellesmere Canal amalgamated with the Chester Canal and the new Birmingham & Liverpool Junction Canal to form the Shropshire Union Railways & Canal Company. Until after the second world war the route from Hurleston to Llangollen was known as the 'Welsh Section' of the Shropshire Union. The term 'Llangollen Canal' didn't gain general currency until British Waterways published a cruising booklet of that name in 1956.

Ellesmere became the headquarters of the canal and the company built imposing offices here. Known as Beech House, these premises still preside over the canal junction but are used residentially now. However, Ellesmere continues to play an important role in the upkeep of the canal, for next door to the old company headquarters is British Waterways Border Counties Maintenance Depot and Office where canal users are welcome to call for advice and information. Many of the structures which comprise this yard date back to the earliest years of the canal. Particularly notable is a handsome stone drydock with a distinctive weathervane in the shape of a narrowboat on its slate roof. Workshops of timber and stone

continued on page 36

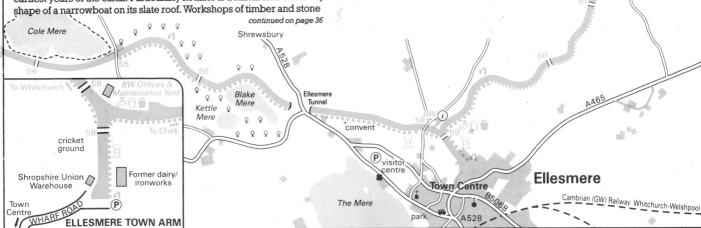

ELLESMERE TOWN ARM

construction include a joiner's shop, blacksmith's forge and pattern store where wooden templates used for making accurate moulds for iron castings are kept. Regretably, rationalisation has reduced the status of the yard. For example, lockgate constrcution, once a regular activity here, is now centralised on Northwich.

Opposite Beech House a short arm diverges from the main line and leads to the terminal wharf of the town itself. At its end a former warehouse still proclaims SHROPSHIRE UNION RAILWAYS & CANAL COMPANY – GENERAL CARRIERS TO CHESTER, LIVERPOOL, MANCHESTER, NORTH & SOUTH STAFFORDSHIRE AND NORTH WALES on its gable end, a tacit reminder of the canal's former importance to the economy of the region. Nowadays the Llangollen Canal swells the community coffers in a different way, and many boaters choose to moor overnight in Ellesmere. The wharf area has been refurbished and turned into an amenity the town can be proud of. One misses, though, the bustle of the cheese creamery, which was up for the sale when we were last in Ellesmere.

East of Ellesmere the canal undertakes a hauntingly lovely journey through Shropshire's own 'Lakeland'. There are seven lakes, or meres, in the neighbourhood of Ellesmere without surface inflow or outflow. They were formed at the end of the Ice Age, 10,000 years ago, as the great glaciers retreated and melted waters collected in cups of the land. The meres support a resident population of birds, including kingfishers, herons, grebe, Canada geese, coots and, naturally, moorhens. In winter there's an influx of wildfowl, including widgeon, teal, pochard, greylag geese and cormorants. On hot late summer evenings the phenomenon of 'breaking' occurs, as algae rise from the depths to spread a deep blue-green veil upon the surface. Cole Mere and Blake Mere both lie beside the canal. Sailing takes place on the former and a charming walk can be had around its perimeter. Blake Mere is only separated from the canal by a narrow belt of trees which provide cool shade for picnics on shirtsleeve days. The unique charm of the meres is evoked in the Shropshire authoress Mary Webb's 1926 novel "Precious Bane".

Navigation Note

Boats cannot pass in Ellesmere Tunnel. Ensure that the way ahead is clear before proceeding.

Ellesmere

Ellesmere is a rare survival: a small, unspoilt country town with no pretensions. Life seems slowly lived here; almost as gently as the rhythm of the waters lapping at the shores of the meres. Visitors – whether they come by car to feed the ducks, or by boat along the Llangollen Canal – are assimilated without the usual symptomatic rash of rubbishy craft shops and frowsy tea rooms. Ellesmere's is a long history, traceable back to the Iron Age, but what the visitor sees today is a turn of the century country town, seemingly preserved in aspic from 20th century expansion. The local economy has been largely an agricultural one. Once there was an ironworks, once there was a railway junction and, more recently, a cheese making creamery. All have gone, and the danger is that Ellesmere may come to rely too much on tourism. Already the local authority have suggested that the dormant creamery by the canal wharf be turned into a museum. Ellesmere's appeal is a subtle magic and they will tamper with it at their peril.

Eating & Drinking

Numerous establishments cater for most tastes. There are, for example, three fish & chip shops; though such a statistic should not be misconstrued; Ellesmere is no Mablethorpe! The following is a subjective selection:
PETE's SANDWICH BAR – Cross Street. Basic cafe notable in that it purveys fresh, hot Vermeulen's pies and pastries.
JUST MILLA'S – Cross Street. Genteel tea rooms above craft shop. Coffees, light lunches and afternoon teas.
NIGHTINGALES – Market Street. Cosy restaurant which won't break the boater's bank.
WHITE HART – Birch Road. Ancient Marstons/Border Brewery house. Bar lunches Thur-Sun. Children welcome.
MILLIES – Birch Road. Wine bar and restaurant housed in 16th century premises. Informal and inexpensive bar menu plus à la carte selection with some vegetarian dishes.

Shopping

Shopping is the pleasantest of experiences in this lovely old town, the highlight, to our mind, being Vermeulen & Sons delicatessen on Cross Street by the town square. Vermeulens open around seven in the morning, by which time the aroma of their fresh baking has wafted itself down to the canal wharf. Their pork pies, still warm to the touch by mid-morning, are made to a unique recipe and are simply irresistible, whilst the cold counter contains a mouthwatering array of glazed meats, pates, shellfish and cheeses. Get them to grind some coffee beans for you and then dare yourself to leave the shop without a box of their fresh cream cakes. Craft and antique shops feature largely throughout the town, so you will do well to cast anchor without some tangible souvenir of Ellesmere and a corresponding deficit in your bank balance. The indoor market, housed in a handsome Victorian pile opposite the post office, operates on Tuesdays and Fridays. Thursday is half-day. There are branches of Lloyds, Midland, Nat-West and TSB banks.

Places to Visit

MERE VISITOR CENTRE – Mereside. Local natural history exhibits and information. Rowing boats are available for hire on the Mere from Cremorne Gardens.

Public Transport

BUSES – regular Crosville service to the interesting border town of Oswestry only quarter of an hour away. Tel: Oswestry (0691) 652402. Irregular buses to Whitchurch and Wem.

T
HE Llangollen Canal traverses a low shelf above a shallow valley watered by the river Perry. The Berwyn and Breidden hills of the Border Marches rise up in the west; blue benign distances or intimidating black tyrants depending on the sky, light and weather. Welsh Frankton, or 'Frankton Junction', became the hub of the Ellesmere Canal system. From two junctions in the form of an H, routes radiated to Pontcysyllte, Ellesmere, Weston Lullingfields (the intended main line to Shrewsbury) and Llanymynech. At Llanymynech there were limestone quarries which brought considerable trade and revenue to the Ellesmere Canal. The canal continued onwards from there as the Montgomeryshire Canal through Welshpool to the mid Wales textile community of Newtown. This route, amounting to some 35 miles from Frankton is now known as the Montgomery Canal. In 1936 a breach occurred where the canal crossed the river Perry by aqueduct and the LMS railway, who had inherited all the canals of the former Shropshire Union, chose not to repair it. Eight years later the canal was legally abandoned. In the ensuing fifty years the Montgomery Canal might well have decayed past the point of return had not its considerable beauty been recognised as the canals underwent a revival for pleasure use.

In 1988 an Act of Parliament was passed effectively reversing the 1944 abandonment Act thus permitting British Waterways and other interested parties to forge ahead with full restoration of the Montgomery Canal. Something like £10 million and perhaps 10 years work will be needed to return the canal to navigation. An isolated 6 mile length near Welshpool has already been restored, and here at Frankton the four locks taking the canal down off the Llangollen were 're-opened' in 1987, though because of water supply problems they are not available for general use as yet. In the meantime the best way to explore the undoubted charms of the Montgomery Canal is on foot. The towpath is in good condition throughout, but a gentle stroll down past the restored locks to the old junction of the Weston line is within the capacity of any Llangollen traveller if only to see what might have been, and to consider how different the fortunes of the canal system of this border region would have been, had the main line made it all the way to Shrewsbury and the Severn.

Between Frankton and New Marton the canal is utterly rural and timelessly remote. Notice how the bridge numbering changes at Frankton; No.70 onwards continuing along the line of the Montgomery Canal, the route to Llangollen recommencing at No.1. There are two locks at New Marton which provide a welcome excuse for some exercise if you are boating. Westbound they are your last; eastbound it's twenty miles to the next ones. At Hindford the Cambrian Railway crosses the canal again (see Map 21). Stopping trains were allowed just half an hour journey time between Hindford and Fenn's Bank. By canal it's a six hour voyage; eloquent enough statistics to explain the waning of the boats with the waxing of the trains.

continued on page 52

Breiddens

Montgomery Canal (under restoration)

River Perry

Weston Branch (derelict)

70

Frankton Locks (restored)

69

Frankton Junction

68

Oswestry
A495

''Narrowboat Inn''

Maestermyn

Welsh Frankton

Ellesmere

½ mile

Hindford

''Jack Myttons''

Henlle

Cambrian (GW) Railway Whitchurch-Welshpool

Berwyn Hills

New Marton Bottom Lock

Lock Cottage

New Marton Top Lock

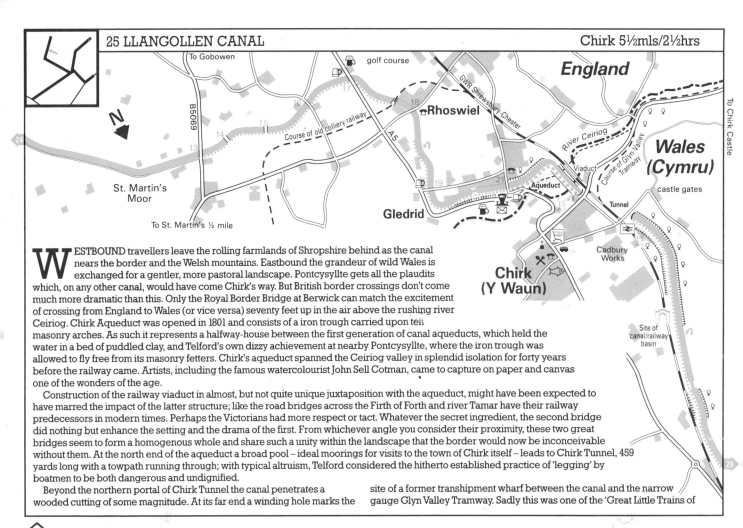

England

To Gobowen

golf course

Rhoswiel

Wales (Cymru)

To Chirk Castle

B5069

N

Course of old colliery railway

GWR Shrewsbury-Chester

River Ceiriog

Course of Glyn Valley Tramway

A5

Viaduct

castle gates

St. Martin's Moor

Gledrid

Aqueduct

Tunnel

To St. Martin's ½ mile

Chirk (Y Waun)

Cadbury Works

Site of canal/railway basin

WESTBOUND travellers leave the rolling farmlands of Shropshire behind as the canal nears the border and the Welsh mountains. Eastbound the grandeur of wild Wales is exchanged for a gentler, more pastoral landscape. Pontcysyllte gets all the plaudits which, on any other canal, would have come Chirk's way. But British border crossings don't come much more dramatic than this. Only the Royal Border Bridge at Berwick can match the excitement of crossing from England to Wales (or vice versa) seventy feet up in the air above the rushing river Ceiriog. Chirk Aqueduct was opened in 1801 and consists of a iron trough carried upon ten masonry arches. As such it represents a halfway-house between the first generation of canal aqueducts, which held the water in a bed of puddled clay, and Telford's own dizzy achievement at nearby Pontcysyllte, where the iron trough was allowed to fly free from its masonry fetters. Chirk's aqueduct spanned the Ceiriog valley in splendid isolation for forty years before the railway came. Artists, including the famous watercolourist John Sell Cotman, came to capture on paper and canvas one of the wonders of the age.

Construction of the railway viaduct in almost, but not quite unique juxtaposition with the aqueduct, might have been expected to have marred the impact of the latter structure; like the road bridges across the Firth of Forth and river Tamar have their railway predecessors in modern times. Perhaps the Victorians had more respect or tact. Whatever the secret ingredient, the second bridge did nothing but enhance the setting and the drama of the first. From whichever angle you consider their proximity, these two great bridges seem to form a homogenous whole and share such a unity within the landscape that the border would now be inconceivable without them. At the north end of the aqueduct a broad pool – ideal moorings for visits to the town of Chirk itself – leads to Chirk Tunnel, 459 yards long with a towpath running through; with typical altruism, Telford considered the hitherto established practice of 'legging' by boatmen to be both dangerous and undignified.

Beyond the northern portal of Chirk Tunnel the canal penetrates a wooded cutting of some magnitude. At its far end a winding hole marks the site of a former transhipment wharf between the canal and the narrow gauge Glyn Valley Tramway. Sadly this was one of the 'Great Little Trains of

Wales' which ran out of steam before the era of railway preservation. The line was built to serve the mines and quarries at the head of the Ceiriog Valley, but passengers were carried too. From a separate station alongside the main line, the track curved precipitously down to the valley floor and then ran beside what is now the B4500, as shown in Eric Leslie's illustration below. The line closed in 1935, had it survived the war it might have been another Talyllyn, especially when one considers that L.T.C. Rolt, a leading light in the rescue of that railway, also held the Glyn Valley Tramway dear to his heart.

Navigation & Mooring

Both the aqueduct and the tunnel at Chirk are wide enough only for one-way working. There are no formal controls, so boaters have to exercise care and patience. Obviously you should not proceed if there is a boat already coming in the opposite direction. Ensure your headlight is working on entering the tunnel. Cruising westbound progress is slowed noticeably by the opposing flow of water, shallowness, and the restricted width of the channel.

A new mooring lay-by in the cutting north of the tunnel can accomodate 3 or 4 boats, but don't expect to watch "Neighbours", reception here is virtually nil. The pool at the southern end of the tunnel has been concrete-lined, but mini-bollards are provided, and this is still, to our mind, a better mooring spot than the cutting.

Chirk

The A5 – Telford's Holyhead Road – makes Chirk a busy border post. All day long the traffic grinds up the hill past the "Croeso i Cymru" signpost, filling the little town with carbon monoxide; an aroma which vies for oxygen space with the pervading fragrance of chocolate from the Cadbury works by the station. Sounds and smells apart, though, Chirk (or Y Waun in Welsh) is an amiable little town worth mooring-up to visit. Nice walks are to be had along the river bank beneath the aqueduct and viaduct.

Eating & Drinking
The HAND HOTEL dominates the centre of the town. It was once a coaching inn and has served generations of border crossers. Pleasure boaters are a relatively new phenomenon, but they are well catered for by an informal buttery. Across the frontier in England lies the BRIDGE INN, reached from the canal at bridge 21 by a steep road. It's a tiny Banks's house offering bar food. Even further out of town, but again canalside by bridge 19, is the NEW INN, another Banks's pub, but considerably larger. Bar and restaurant meals are available and there's a garden and a payphone. Chirk itself also has two cafes and a fish & chip shop.

Shopping
There's a good choice of shops including: Co-op stores, butcher, newsagent, chemist, bakery, Midland Bank and a well stocked Welsh craft shop. All are located in the town centre not much more than 5 minutes walk from either end of the tunnel.

Places to Visit
CHIRK CASTLE – 1½ miles west of north end of tunnel.

Open Wed, Thur, Sat & Sun afternoons plus Bank Holidays May – Sep inclusive. Admission charge. It's a long but worthwhile walk from the canal to this 600 years old Marcher fortress now under the auspices of the National Trust. The astonishingly ornate entrance gates are much nearer the canal.

Public Transport
BUSES – Hourly Crosville service to/from Wrexham and Oswestry. Tel: Wrexham (0978) 261361. Towpath walkers will be more interested in the Bryn Melyn Motors service to/from Llangollen via Froncysyllte. Tel: Llangollen (0978) 860701.

TRAINS – Fairly regular services to/from Chester and Shrewsbury offering, southbound from Chirk, a bird's eye view of the adjacent aqueduct! Tel: Shrewsbury (0743) 64041.

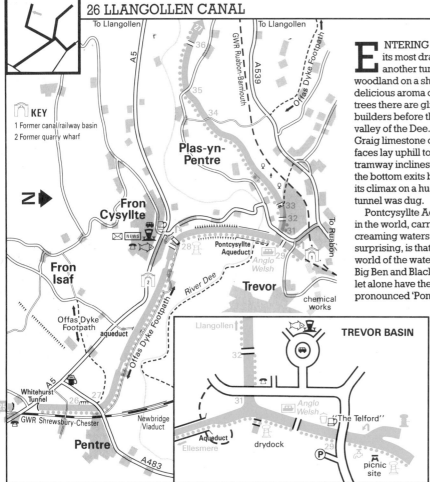

KEY
1 Former canal/railway basin
2 Former quarry wharf

E NTERING Offa's Dyke country, the Llangollen Canal prepares to make its most dramatic gesture. But first westbound travellers are treated to another tunnel followed by an enchanted journey through a mask of woodland on a shelf above the river Dee. Given the right conditions, the delicious aroma of pinewood fills the air. Between the ivy clad boles of the tall trees there are glimpses of an impressive railway viaduct. Like the canal builders before them, the railway engineers had to contend with the deep valley of the Dee. On the outskirts of 'Fron' the remains of the former Pen-Y-Graig limestone quarries are evident alongside the canal. The actual quarry faces lay uphill to the west and the stone was brought down by a series of tramway inclines on wagons. The tops of six lime kilns were at road level with the bottom exits beside the canal. Passing lift bridge 28 the canal approaches its climax on a huge embankment built from spoil excavated when Chirk tunnel was dug.

Pontcysyllte Aqueduct, quite the most astonishing feat of canal engineering in the world, carries the canal one hundred and twenty feet high across the creaming waters of the river Dee. Superlatives are superfluous, but what is surprising, is that the aqueduct is relatively unknown beyond the narrow world of the waterways. It ought to be of chocolate box familiarity along with Big Ben and Blackpool Tower, and yet few people are aware of its existence, let alone have the ability to get their teeth around its knotty consonants. But, pronounced 'Pont-ker-sulth-tee', the bare facts are that it is over 1,000 feet long, 127 feet tall at its deepest point, and consists of an iron trough supported by 19 stone piers. The aqueduct was completed in 1805, the year of Nelson's death at Trafalgar. Along with the Clifton and Menai Straits suspension bridges, it is ranked amongst Telford's outstanding achievements.

At Trevor the canal was to have to have carried on up and over the ridge now occupied by the huge Monsanto chemical plant, and then down through Wrexham to the Dee at Chester. Such a course would have required many locks, a very long tunnel, or a series of boat lifts. The enormity of this undertaking, coupled with the recession which occured as an aftermath to the Naploenic Wars, thwarted the Ellesmere Canal Company's plans to

continued on page 45

Telford's two extremes.
This page: Pontcysyllte Aqueduct, Llangollen Canal.
Opposite: Nantwich Aqueduct, Shropshire Union Canal.

The shape of things to come?
Newly restored locks at Frankton, Montgomery Canal.

continued from page 40

provide a direct canal between the Mersey and the Severn. Telford and his associates would doubtless have overcome the terrain in time, but financially the outlay involved would have broken the bank. In place of the envisaged main line northwards, the canal beyond the aqueduct terminated at a transhipment wharf from where, first a tramway, then later a railway, connected with quarries and collieries on the higher ground in the direction of Ruabon. A further arm described an arc to the east serving chemical, pottery and ironworks in the vicinity. In the Ellesmere Canal's commercial heyday much traffic was therefore generated in the neighbourhood.

Ironically, a canal to Llangollen was not in the original Ellesmere Canal Company scheme of things. Only when it became apparent that the main line would never be completed, did the company's thoughts turn to the provision of a feeder from the river Dee at Llantisilio to the canal at Trevor. It was a necessary but difficult project, for the cutting of a canal along the precipitous slopes of the Vale of Llangollen held considerable problems. In the event it was the last section of the canal to be completed, over two years after the aqueduct had been opened to traffic. Technicalities apart, it is one of the most memorable lengths of canal in the country, an aquatic mountain odyssey of unparalleled loveliness.

Navigation & Mooring

There is one-way working only over Pontcysyllte Aqueduct. Do not proceed until it is clear of oncoming craft. There is no guard rail on the non-towpath side of the aqueduct, so ensure that children and pets are under rigorous control as you make the crossing.

The 'quietest' moorings at Trevor are to be found beyond bridge 29 in the old transhipment basin. They get very busy mid-week in the summer. Fron Cysyllte makes a pleasant alternative, with just as many facilities close by.

Froncysyllte

A mountain goat of a village with, now that we are in Wales, its to be expected sprinkling of Nonconformist chapels. If your legs are up to it it's worth following the zig-zagging lane up to the crest of the ridge for spectacular views across the Dee Valley and up into the Vale of Llangollen.

Eating & Drinking

THE AQUEDUCT – adjacent bridge 28. A Marston's/ Border pub offering light snacks and a cosy fire. Children are welcome and there's a panoramic view across to the aqueduct.
Good fish & chip shop on main road.

Shopping

Post office stores, and small newsagent (opens after 9am when the proprietor gets back from his delivery round!)

Public Transport

BUSES – Useful and fairly regular Bryn Melyn services to/ from Chirk and Llangollen. Tel: Llangollen 0978 860701.

Trevor

Industry spills down the hillside and pastel painted semis border the basin. A large car park reflects the growing popularity of the aqueduct as a venue for motorists, and

picnic tables are provided by the old transhipment basin. A swooping by-road leads down to the old stone bridge across the Dee from which one of the most dramatic views of Pontcysyllte is to be gained.

Eating & Drinking

THE TELFORD – licensed restaurant adjacent to canal basin. Bar & restaurant meals, children welcome. Tel: Llangollen 820469.
Fish & chips nearby.

Shopping

General stores with off licence 200 yards from the basin.

Public Transport

BUSES – Hourly Crosville service to/from Llangollen and Wrexham. Tel: Wrexham (0978) 261361.

Boatyard & Hire Base

TREVOR WHARF SERVICES – Trevor, Llangollen, Clwyd LL20 7TX. Tel: Llangollen (0978) 821749. Pumpout, diesel, Shell gas, repairs & servicing, drydock, crane/lift-out, souvenir shop, day-boat hire.
ANGLO WELSH WATERWAY HOLIDAYS – Canal Basin, Market Harborough, Leics LE16 7BJ. Tel: MH (0858) 466910. 2 to 10 berth hire craft.

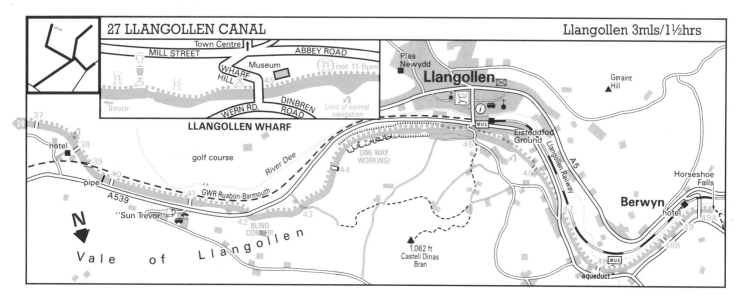

AFTER the high drama of Pontcysyllte you might have expected the last lap into Llangollen to be something of an anticlimax. Happily, this is not the case: rather, the canal treats you to all the wild majesty that the celebrated Vale of Llangollen can muster. Great buttresses of limestone cliffs tower above conifer plantations, making Hurleston and gentle green Cheshire seem a long way away. When the weather is kind one is constantly lifting one's eyes up into the hills where sunlight gives the bright heather ridges the clarity of well executed marquetry. But Wales wouldn't be Wales if it weren't for the frequent, dripping Celtic mists that come creeping up the valley of the Dee, Welsh *hiwyls* which muffle boat exhausts and dampen the woods, if not the spirits.

Not altogether surprisingly, the section between Trevor and Llangollen has a history of breaches. In 1945 the bank collapsed by bridge 41 and the adjoining railway was swept away. A goods train plunged into the gap and the driver was killed. Bursts occurred more frequently thereafter and by the middle Eighties it became apparent to British Waterways engineers that this section would have, effectively to be rebuilt. Now the canal bed has

been concrete-lined, under-drained and fitted with a waterproof membrane as part of a £5 million rolling programme of improvements between Chirk and Llangollen.

Never exactly wide, the canal narrows as it approaches Llangollen and at busy times boaters have to exercise more than a little restraint and patience. Running above the grey roofs of the town the canal reaches the old Llangollen wharf where the warehouse has been refurbished as a canal centre, museum and base for the horse-drawn boats which ply the final, narrow, shallow section up to Horseshoe Falls. A winding hole beyond the warehouse marks the turning point for all powered craft. Then, accompanied by the river and the restored steam railway, the feeder canal continues for a couple of miles beyond Llangollen to Llantisilio. In many ways it seems quite apt that boaters should have to stretch their legs to reach what amounts to the end – but is really the beginning! – of the canal. Horseshoe Falls, though, with its great crescent shaped weir, is a point of pilgrimmage not to be eschewed. Here, by the tiny valve house which meters the flow of water into the canal, it is time to savour the forty-four mile journey from Hurleston, to recall affectionately the pastures of the Cheshire Plain; the locks at Grindley Brook; the strange Mosses; the gently lapping Meres; the bold, bare mountains; and the high aqueducts: all the ingredients, in fact, which taken together, make the Llangollen one of the great inland waterway experiences in the world.

Navigation Note
Between Trevor and Llangollen – and especially west of bridge 41 – the canal is narrow and shallow. There are three short lengths where it is impossible to pass oncoming craft and, in the absence of any formal control (such as a timetable for single direction flow) considerable tact and restraint is required. Matters are exacerbated by the shortage of moorings at Llangollen, and by mid-week – when all the outward bound hire boats converge on Llangollen – chaos often ensues as one set of boats is trying to reach Llangollen as another is attempting to leave. Whilst we would not dispute the satisfaction of reaching the town by boat, there is much to be said for mooring at Trevor and walking into Llangollen along the towpath or catching the bus. Alternatively, if it fits in with your travelling pattern, try and cruise from Trevor to Llangollen very early or very late in the day when other boats are less likely to be on the move.

Llangollen

Once a year in early July, this little grey-slated Welsh town takes on a cosmopolitan atmosphere, as singers and dancers in colourful national dress take part in the famous Eisteddfod. In fact the town bustles with tourists all summer long, as it has done since the 18th century, when early travel writers like Hazlitt and Borrow discovered the wild charm of the Vale of Llangollen. The canal wharf lies over the river from the bulk of the town, but it's just a short walk across the graceful Bishop Trevor Bridge to the centre.

Eating & Drinking

Llangollen has more than its fair share of uninspiring cafes and pubs, but there are several excellent eating and drinking places too. We would certainly recommend GALES on Bridge Street, an atmospheric wine bar with an imaginative menu and a pleasing cross section of clientel; in fact hardly a Yuppie in sight! For a more formal, yet intimate meal, book a table at CAESARS on the south end of the river bridge; reservations can be made on Llangollen 860133. The ROYAL HOTEL opposite, is a Trust House Forte establishment with a choice of bars and restaurants. If all you need is a decent pint of bitter then try some Boddingtons' at the BULL INN on Castle Street in the centre of the town, or some Robinsons at the BRIDGE END just below the canal wharf. One other pub worth noting is the SUN TREVOR, canalside by bridge 41, a comfortable free house, offering bar and restaurant meals.

Shopping

Predictably there's a surfeit of gift shops, and you'll have no trouble finding a doll in Welsh costume to take home for your auntie. In amongst all the dross, however, are some genuinely attractive local crafts. LLANGOLLEN WEAVERS are a prime example, housed in a 13th century mill overlooking the Dee. Demonstrations of weaving are given on 150 years old looms and the resultant fabrics and clothes are on sale in the mill shop. There are some good food shops as well, like the COLLEGE BAKERY and JAMES BAILEY'S delicatessen with its charming staff and delicious baking; both can be found on Castle Street. Market day is Tuesday and early closing Thursday. There are branches of Barclays, NatWest and Midland banks.

Places to Visit

TOURIST INFORMATION CENTRE – Town Hall. Tel: Llangollen (0978) 860828.
CANAL EXHIBITION CENTRE – The Wharf. Tel: Llangollen 860702. Open daily Easter – September. Admission charge. Fascinating little museum celebrating the history of the canals housed in former warehouse. Souvenir shop. Horse-drawn, canvas-covered, open boats ply (as they have done since 1884) from the museum along the canal feeder to Pentrefelin on a 45 minute return trip; daily in July and August, otherwise weekends only.
LLANGOLLEN RAILWAY – station riverside, adjacent canal wharf. Tel: Llangollen (0978) 860951/860979. Daily summer service of mostly steam hauled trains to Berwyn (for Horseshoe Falls) and Deeside Halt; round trip 50 minutes. Locomotive stud includes a pair of GWR 'Manor' class of the sort which travelled the line in its heyday.
PLAS NEWYDD – Butler Hill. Tel: Llangollen 860828. Open daily 1st May – 30th September. Admission charge. This gorgeous black & white timbered house set in charming gardens was the home of the 'Ladies of Llangollen', two daughters of aristocratic Irish families who lived here from 1779 to 1831. They were the talk of the neighbourhood and counted amongst their acquaintances some of the great men of the period. Wordsworth, Sir Walter Scott and the Duke of Wellington all stayed at Plas Newydd.

In addition to the above attractions, the Llangollen area is particularly good for walking in. Two obvious destinations are the Horseshoe Falls, which can be reached by following the canal feeder towpath west from bridge 45, and Castell Dinas Bran a summit of over 1,000ft topped by a ruined castle, signposted footpaths lead from bridge 45.

Public Transport

BUSES – Crosville services: east to Wrexham and Chester, west to Corwen and Bala. Tel: Wrexham (0978) 261361. Local Bryn Melyn services to Chirk. Tel: Llangollen (0978) 860701.

TO SUBCONSCIOUSLY RELEGATE the Middlewich Branch to the back of your mind as an unspectacular, but necessary link in the waterways of the North-west would be unjust, for this is a rumbustious canal, carrying you loftily above the snaking valley of the river Weaver, presenting you with expansive views towards a horizon bounded by Delamere Forest and the Peckforton Hills. Church Minshull – all russett brick and black & white half timbering – looks wistfully, from the canal's elevated position, like a toy village embracing the river's banks. Down there, somewhere, the map suggests – and you may catch glimpses of it through the thick woodlands – is an expanse of water known as 'Top Flash', a

subsidence induced lake beside the Weaver; a river which becomes navigable downstream at Winsford, and indeed used regularly by sea-going vessels as far inland as Anderton .

Well-to-do farms border the canal: their fields filled with big milking herds or cut red by the plough in a ruddy shade of corduroy. The main London - Glasgow railway crosses the canal, its electric trains swishing by at thirty times your speed. To the South-east lies a forgotten, older transport route: a Roman road which linked the early salt mines at Nantwich and Middlewich.

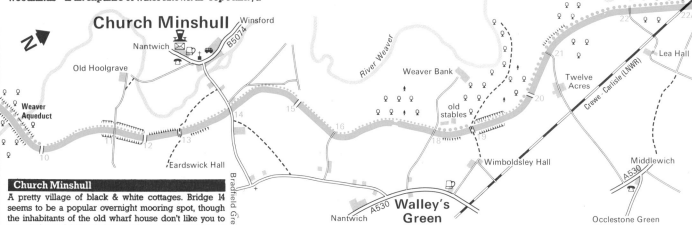

Church Minshull

A pretty village of black & white cottages. Bridge 14 seems to be a popular overnight mooring spot, though the inhabitants of the old wharf house don't like you to moor in front of their windows, and who can blame them? Reader's of L.T.C. Rolt's "Narrow Boat" will recognise Minshull as the village where the Rolts enjoyed an extended stay in the fateful autumn of 1939. Rolt revelled in the close-knit community that flourished here: the blacksmith who shod the local cart horses; and the miller whose water wheels supplied the village with electricity right up until 1960. But the 'tide of black tarmacadam' which had only just covered the cobbled sets of the main

street brought with it many changes which would have broken Rolt's heart. Why not walk back via Old Hoolgrave and bridge 11, a pleasant alternative to the main road.

Eating & Drinking
THE BADGER – historic pub in village centre, Les Routiers recommended. Tetley's, bar and restaurant meals, garden and games room.

Shopping
Post office stores (behind pub) off licence and newspapers as well. Open Mon-Sat (half day on Wed) and Sun am.

Public Transport
BUSES – hourly Mon-Sat to/from Crewe and Northwich. Tel: Crewe (0270) 505350.

KEY
Sites of former salt works

Congleton

Lostock Gralam

Big Lock

Middlewich Locks

Kings Lock

Town Centre

Middlewich N' Boats

Wardle Lock

Middlewich

Aqueduct

Middlewich Manor

Stanthorne Lock

River Wheelock

Andersen

SUC Middlewich Branch

Winsford rly sta 1 mile

Glasgow

London

Nantwich

Trent & Mersey Canal to Kidsgrove

MIDDLEWICH WAS ALWAYS a centre of boating activity in commercial carrying days, and remains busy now with pleasure boaters, situated, as it is, on both the Cheshire Ring and Four Counties Ring, two of the most popular cruising circuits. A pair of busy boatyards and hire bases add to the through traffic, making a walk down Middlewich Locks something of a gongoozlers paradise. The three central locks are all deep, and total over 30ft in depth. A drydock adjoins the upper intermediate pound. Now used by Middlewich Narrowboats, it once formed part of Seddons saltworks basin. Seddons had their own fleet of narrowboats for bringing in coal from north Staffordshire and for taking finished salt to the Mersey ports. They were still using horses to haul the boats in the Fifties, but the fleet was broken up in 1960 and the works closed a few years later.

Big Lock, like Croxton Aqueduct to the north, was built to wide beam dimensions in the anticipation that Mersey 'flats' would trade to Middlewich. But, inexplicably, the tunnels north of Anderton were constructed too narrow to take such craft, so no wide beam barges ever used this section in practice. Alongside the lock chamber, the gates of which used to be operated by curious drum and chain machinery, stands a handsome pub of the same name. Nearby is a modern textile works.

Middlewich

A salt town since Roman times - there are relics on display in the library - Middlewich has undergone much change in recent years as the old steaming pan method of manufacture has given way to the modern vacuum. Thus the forest of chimney stacks which once held up the Middlewich sky have all tumbled, but the sturdy tower of St Michael's parish church - scarred by missiles of a battle during the Civil War - still looms over the rooftops, adding character to this now placid little town which repays closer inspection.

Eating & Drinking

Pubs are plentiful and the variety of beer on offer wide, Middlewich seemingly being on the frontiers of a number of brewery empires large and small: Robinsons, Marstons, Wilsons and Tetleys being amongst those available. Prominent canalside pubs include: KINGS LOCK, canalside bridge 167, Tetleys, food, garden; NEWTON BREWERY, overlooking canal north of bridge 172, Marstons, food, garden; and BIG LOCK, alongside its namesake, a quiet Tetley house which usually has some sort of food available. Fish & chip shops are sprinkled liberally through the town; the handiest being slap bang by Kings Lock.

Shopping

The shops of Middlewich are old-fashioned in an unself-conscious way and this is a pleasant spot to re-stock the galley. However, it says much for the age in which we live that VERNONS once exquisite butchers has been turned into a video shop. There are NatWest and Barclays banks in Wheelock Street. Early closing is on Wednesdays.

Public Transport

BUSES – services to Crewe, Sandbach etc depart from the Bull Ring by the church. Tel: Chester (0244) 602666.

Boatyards & Hire Bases

ANDERSEN BOATS – Wych House Lane, Lewin Street, Middlewich CW10 9QB. Tel: Middlewich (060684) 3668. 4 to 10 berth hire craft (Hoseasons). Pumpout and Calor gas.

MIDDLEWICH NARROWBOATS – Canal Terrace, Middlewich CW10 9BD. Tel: Middlewich (060684) 2460. 4 to 12 berth hire craft. Pumpout, Elsan & rubbish disposal, water, diesel, Calor gas, repairs & servicing, drydock, chandlery, gifts, provisions and laundry facilities.

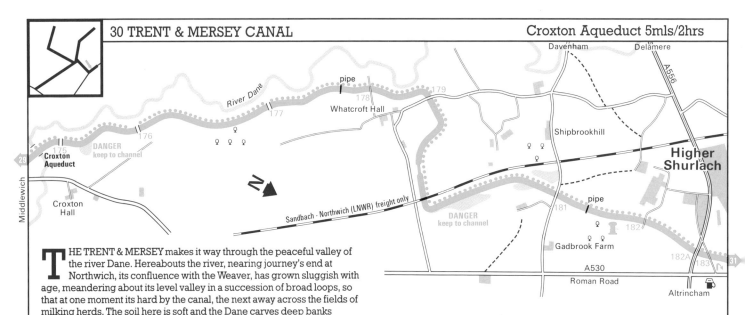

THE TRENT & MERSEY makes it way through the peaceful valley of the river Dane. Hereabouts the river, nearing journey's end at Northwich, its confluence with the Weaver, has grown sluggish with age, meandering about its level valley in a succession of broad loops, so that at one moment its hard by the canal, the next away across the fields of milking herds. The soil here is soft and the Dane carves deep banks shadowed by alder and willow. Croxton aqueduct carries the canal across the river.

Along this rural length of the Trent & Mersey there are three broad expanses of water bordering the canal. Do not let your curiosity tempt you from the main channel, for these flashes, caused by subsidence, are filled with the submerged wrecks of abandoned barges and narrowboats; an inland waterway equivalent of Scapa Flow. Many of the narrowboats were brought here and sunken en masse during the Fifties in circumstances almost as controversial in canal terms as the scuttling of the German Fleet at Scapa after the First World War. In what was probably a book-keeping exercise, British Waterways rid themselves of surplus narrowboats in this fashion in a number of watery graves throughout the system. Recently, some of the better preserved wrecks have been raised and taken away for restoration and preservation. One generation's cast-offs become the next's prized possessions.

The Trent & Mersey Canal was completed in 1777. Prime-movers behind its promotion were the pottery manufacturers of North Staffordshire. These gentlemen desperately wanted a more reliable method of transport, than the then unchallenged packhorse, for the carriage of raw materials, such as clay from Cornwall and flint from Sussex (both commodities making the long sea voyage round to the Mersey ports), and the export of finished goods to the growing markets of Europe and North America. James Brindley engineered the route, which measured 92 miles from Preston Brook in the north to Shardlow in the south, as part of his scheme for a 'Grand Cross' of canal routes linking the four great English estuaries of Mersey, Humber, Thames and Severn. The Company's Latin motto was suitably pompous: *Pro Patriam Populumque Fluit,* It Flows for Country and People. Brindley wanted it to be known as the 'Grand Trunk Canal', a name which subsequently gained currency amongst working boatmen.

KEY
Sites of former salt works

Marbury Country Park

Clare Cruisers

pipe

Original Course of Canal

Marston New Cut

Great Budworth

B5075

Marston

New Cheshire salt works

Pickmere

BP

Northwich

Wincham

Wincham Brook

Northwich 1½ miles

A559

Aqueduct

Altrincham

Wincham Wharf

Chester - Manchester (CLC)

ICI Lostock Works

A530

BW Depot

Anderton Lift

Anderton

ICI Winnington Works

Weaver Navigation to Northwich and Winsford

Northwich

ICI lagoons

B5082

Broken Cross

Middlewich

SIBERIA SPRINGS flippantly to mind when we think of salt, but Britain's own salt industry was centred on this area of Cheshire, and the landscape through which the canal winds betrays every influence of this activity, past and present. Apart from the trade it created for the canal, the salt industry's greatest effect on the waterway lay unfortunately in the amount of subsidence it invoked; as relatively recently as 1958 a new length of canal had to be built to by-pass a section near Marston particularly troubled by instability.

Anderton Boat Lift dates from 1875. It was designed by Sir Edward Leader Williams, an eminent Victorian engineer also responsible for the Barton Swing Aqueduct near Manchester. The lift was constructed to bridge the 50ft disparity between the Trent & Mersey and the Weaver Navigation below. A massive iron framework supports two water-filled caissons, each of which can carry a pair of narrowboats. Originally hydraulically powered by steam, since early this century the structure has been electrically operated using a system of counterbalance weights.

Tragically, this great monument to our canal heritage has been unworkable since 1983. However a Development Group has ambitious proposals, including a visitor centre and other associated attractions which, in the long term they hope will provide sufficient momentum of interest and associated use for the lift to be fully restored.

Weaver Navigation to Weston Point and MSC

to Preston Brook

Anderton

Eating & Drinking
STANLEY ARMS – overlooks The Lift. Greenall's, bar meals, family room, garden with playground, putting and bowling greens. THE MOORINGS – Anderton Marina (ABC). Restaurant and coffee shop. Table bookings on Northwich (0606) 79789. Also gift shop, maps, guides etc.

Boatyards & Hire Bases
ALVECHURCH BOAT CENTRES – Scarfield Wharf, Alvechurch, Worcestershire B48 7SQ. Tel: 021-445 2909. 2 to 12 berth craft (Blue Riband Club). Pumpout, Elsan disposal, water, diesel, Calor gas, moorings, slipway and other facilities. Boatyard telephone – Northwich 79642.

CLARE CRUISERS – Uplands Road Basin, Anderton, Northwich CW9 6AJ. Tel: Northwich (0606) 77199. 2 to 12 berth hire craft (Hoseasons). Pumpout, diesel, water, Calor gas, rubbish disposal, servicing & repairs, maps and guides.

Marston & Wincham

Eating & Drinking
THE SALT BARGE – adjacent bridge 193. Greenall's, bar food and garden with childrens play area.
BRINDLEYS – adjacent bridge 189. Coffees, teas, bar and restaurant meals in handsome canal warehouse conversion.

Boatyard
WINCHAM WHARF – Manchester Road, Lostock Gralam, Northwich CW9 7NT. Tel: Northwich (0606) 48354. Pumpout, Elsan disposal, diesel, repairs & servicing, boatbuilding, drydock and other facilities. Day and trip boats for hire and charter.

Continued from Map 8

market days and the town is at its liveliest then. Browsing from stall to stall, you'll find the meat and dairy produce outlets particularly excellent. Browns in the High Street is an old fashioned provisions merchant specialising in local dairy and meat produce, Potteries oatcakes, pikelets and gingerbread. Other facilties include: branches of all the main banks, a launderette in Shropshire Street and supermarkets. There are several antique shops and a good secondhand book shop. Mongers is a delightful little sweet shop at the extremity of Cheshire Street. The town centre is about 15 minutes walk from the canal, slightly closer at hand there's a general store and newsagent open daily.

Public Transport
BUSES – services to/from Stoke and Shrewsbury, Mon-Sat. Tel: Stoke (0782) 747000. For local services telephone Telford (0952) 291300.

Boatyard & Hire Base
HOLIDAYS AFLOAT – The Boatyard, Market Drayton, Shropshire. Tel: MD (0630) 2641. 3 to 6 berth hire craft.

Continued from Map 24

Whittington
Eating & Drinking
THE NARROWBOAT INN – canalside bridge 5. Modern purpose built pub owned by adjacent boatyard. Bass, Ruddles and regular guest beers. Bar meals, inexpensive Sunday lunches a speciality. Children welcome.

Boatyard & Hire Base
MAESTERMYN HIRE CRUISERS & WELSH LADY CRUISERS – Ellesmere Road, Whittington, Oswestry, Shropshire. Tel: Oswestry (0691) 662424. 2 to 9 berth hire craft (former Blakes, latter Hoseasons). Pumpout, water, diesel, Elsan & rubbish disposal, gas, repairs & servicing, boatbuilding, slipway, groceries, chandlery, souvenirs and Sunday papers. Payphone.

Hindford
Eating & Drinking
THE JACK MYTTON INN & RESTAURANT – canalside bridge 11. Separate formal and informal restaurants, children's menu in latter. Tel: (0691) 662327.

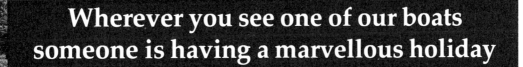

Wherever you see one of our boats someone is having a marvellous holiday

110 luxury narrowboats, with an average age of only 3 years, from 2-12 berths operating from 4 bases, **Alvechurch**, **Birmingham**, **Anderton** and **Gayton**, with a wide choice of canal and river cruising. Short breaks and 10/11 night holidays a speciality.

Write, phone or call for a free colour brochure:
Alvechurch Boat Centres, Scarfield Wharf, Alvechurch, Nr. Birmingham, Worcestershire. B48 7SQ. Tel: 021-445-2909

Information

How to Use the Maps

There are thirty-one numbered maps. Maps 1 to 17 cover the 'main line' of the Shropshire Union Canal between Autherley Junction (Wolverhampton) and Ellesmere Port. Numbers 18 to 27 cover the Llangollen Canal from Hurleston Junction (Nantwich) to the Horseshoe Falls (Llangollen). Numbers 28 to 31 cover the Middlewich Branch of the Shropshire Union together with the Trent & Mersey Canal between Middlewich and Anderton (Northwich). An arrow at the edge of each map indicates the following map number to refer to. A 'thumbnail' map at the top left hand corner of each map indicates your overall position. Figures quoted at the top of each map refer to the distance and average cruising time for that particular page. Obviously, cruising times vary with the nature of your boat and the number of crew at your disposal to work the locks, so these quoted times should be taken only as an estimate.

Using the Text

Each map is accompanied by a commentary on the route of the canal, describing the sort of landscape it passes through, something of its history and making the occasional wry comment or two. More often than not this appears above the map itself, but where more space is needed it follows on the next page. Brief portraits of canalside towns and villages are given together with itemised or summarised information on facilities.

Eating & Drinking. Pubs, restaurants, cafes, fish & chip shops and other fast food outlets considered to be of interest to canal users are listed. In towns and cities a selection has obviously to be made, so we try to list a cross section of establishments likely to appeal to different tastes and budgets. We don't set out to make judgements in the 'Egon Ronay' sense but, generally speaking, the more detail we give the better (we think!) the establishment is. Please bear in mind, however, that such places can rapidly change from being well-appointed and attentive to being run-down and indifferent. Let us know of any disappointments you have, and we'll think twice about entering them in the next edition. Conversely, if you find anywhere good that we have managed to miss, then tell us!

Shopping. Shopping in unfamiliar towns and villages is one of the great pleasures of a canal holiday. In the case of larger places we try to give an impression of the style and nature of facilities available, mentioning any particularly interesting or charming shops which caught our eye. Whilst, with regard to villages, we list what's available in basic detail and try to give some idea of opening hours. Locating shops is made easy by reference to the symbols on the maps.

Places to Visit. Details are given in this category of Tourist Information Centres, museums, visitor centres, stately homes etc likely to be of interest to users of this guide.

Public Transport. Useful details for towpath walkers planning one-way walks or boaters planning an excursion ashore. Always try and check with the relevant operator; bus services are especially prone to change.

Boatyards & Hire Bases. Every boatyard and hire base is marked on the relevant map and listed appropriately. It is not practical for us to quote any indication of quality and cost applicable to hire fleets. However, we recommend that prospective hirers obtain a selection of brochures from a cross section of bases and agencies before making a firm booking.

Walking

Towpaths are the property of British Waterways and, though not always specifically 'rights of way', are open to the general public, no licence or permit being required for use by walkers. Cyclists, however, are not allowed to ride along towpaths without a special permit from British Waterways. Difficulty of access and poor conditions have been twin factors instrumental in discouraging people from walking along towpaths for recreation in the past, but local authorities have done much to remove these hazards in recent times. As well as boating along the canals to do our research, we also walk the towpaths a good deal; indeed one often gains more enjoyment and insight from canal exploration by 'Shank's Pony' than when having to concentrate on managing a boat. But our reconnaisance trips have allowed us from personal experience to categorise the towpath into three standards. 'Good' can usually be taken to indicate a firm, wide and dry base. 'Adequate' hints at the chance of mud and vegetation, but can be considered passable. 'Poor' reflects conditions not conducive to enjoyable walking; a challenge for die-hards, but not much fun for a family stroll.

Boating

Boating on inland waterways is an established, though relatively small facet of the UK holiday industry. There are over 20,000 privately owned boats registered on the canals. In addition to this there are numerous firms offering boats for hire. They range from small operators with half a dozen boats or so to sizeable fleets run by companies with several bases. Size, though, is not necessarily an accurate barometer of quality. Nowadays most hire boats have all the creature comforts you are likely to expect: double beds, flushing loos, showers, fridges, cookers etc etc.

Traditionally, hire craft are booked out by the week or fortnight; though an increasing number of firms advertise short breaks of two, three of four days, particularly in the spring and autumn. All reputable hire firms give newcomers tuition in boat handling, lock working and general navigation, and it is considerably easier than learning to ride a bicycle, or drive a car. Canal boating holidays are enjoyed by many thousands of people every year. They make ideal holidays for families or groups of friends. Age should not be considered a barrier as long as one is relatively fit. It may sound glib and cliched, but boating really is the ideal way of slowing down.

Navigational Advice

Locks. Locks are part of the fun of canal boating holidays, but they are potentially dangerous environments for careless adults, children and pets. Use of them should be methodical and unhurried, whilst special care should be taken in rain, frost and snow when slippery hazards abound. Most of the locks included in this guide are of the standard narrow variety, but north of Nantwich on the Shropshire Union route to Chester are widebeam and capable of fitting two narrowboats side by side. There are 'staircase' locks at Bunbury (Map 13) and Grindley Brook (Map 20). Here, adjacent chambers share common gates. When working uphill, the upper chamber must be full so that the water in it can be released to fill the lower chamber. Going downhill, the lower chamber must be empty to enable the water from the upper chamber to flow into it.

Lift Bridges. Lift bridges are an engaging feature of the Llangollen Canal. Many are now modern metal structures operated with the use of a lock windlass. There are, however, a number of the original wooden built structures still in use operated by counter balance weights. Some are equipped with chains which it is necessary to pull down on to cause the platform to rise. Occasionally they seem to have 'lost' their chains and one has to improvise by either propping the platform up with a boat shaft, or throwing a rope over the balance beam. In either case great care should be taken to ensure that the platform remains firmly upright as your boat passes through.

Private Navigations. The British Waterways canals covered in this guide connect with two independently owned navigations: the Manchester Ship Canal at Ellesmere Port (Map 17) and the River Dee at Chester (Map 16). In the normal course of events hire boat operators are unlikely to permit holidaymakers to enter either of these waterways. Private boat owners face several bureaucratic and navigational hurdles to gain access to the MSC or the Dee, though once these are surmounted the experience is likely to be just reward for their persistence. In the case of the Manchester Ship Canal pleasure craft must comply with a series of conditions such as Third Party insurance and a Certificate of Seaworthiness. Details of these and other relevant matters can be obtained from the MSC Company at Collier Street, Runcorn, Cheshire WA7 1HA. Tel: Runcorn (0928) 580083.

The Dee below Chester is a tidal, fast flowing river not recommended for use by canal craft. However, the Upper Dee flows charmingly through the Cheshire countryside and can be reached via the Dee Branch from Tower Wharf and by passage over a weir upstream of the Old Dee Bridge. Advance warning to use the Dee Branch must be given to British Waterways on Chester (0244) 390372. Silt tends to collect below the bottom gates of the final lock and this will need to be flushed away before you can gain access to the river. Passage to the Upper Dee must be made an hour either side of high tide as it involves the use of a gate in the aformentioned weir. Use of the gate must be arranged with the North West Water Authority on 051-339 6262. Finally, having reached the comparative calm of the Upper Dee a licence to navigate this part of the river must be obtained from Chester City Council. Telephone Chester (0244) 340144 for further details.

Closures. Closures, or in waterway parlance, 'stoppages', usually occur between November and April when maintenance work is undertaken. Occasionally an emergency stoppage may take place at short notice, closing part of the route you intend to cruise. Up to date details are available to hire boaters from their hire base. Alternatively, British Waterways operate a recorded message telephone service for private boaters detailing emergency stoppages on 071-723 8486.

Amendments. You may be interested to know that we can supply amendment sheets for the Canal Companion series. These give up to date details of any changes of importance which have occurred since publication. Private orders supplied direct from us receive these automatically, but we are happy to supply them independently on receipt of an SAE and request for the sheet(s) you require. Please note, though, that the amendment sheet is only relevant to the latest edition of each Companion!

Societies

The Inland Waterways Association was founded in 1946 to campaign for the retention of the canal system, and many of the routes open for pleasure boating today might not have been available but for this organisation. You can become a member of the IWA and meet kindred spirits as well as contributing to the waterways movement. alternatively you might consider joining the Shropshire Union Canal Society which maintains close links with the Shropshire Union, Llangollen and Montgomery canals. The Boat Museum at Ellesmere Port also has an affiliated supporter's group. up to date details of the IWA and these other societies can be obtained from: Inland Waterways Association, 114 Regent's Park Road, London NW1 8UQ. Tel: 071-586 2556.

Useful Contacts

British Waterways are organised on a regional basis. The canals covered in this Companion belong mostly to the North West Region. Their head office address is:

British Waterways
Navigation Road
Northwich
Cheshire CW8 1BH.
Tel: Northwich (0606) 74321.

A group of Waterway Managers are responsible for individual sections of the canals. They welcome enquiries from the general public, either by telephone or by calling in during office hours.

British Waterways
Shropshire Union Canal
(Autherley – Audlem)
Norbury Junction
Stafford ST20 0PN
Tel: Stafford (0785) 74253

British Waterways
Shropshire Union Canal
(Audlem – Ellesmere Port & Middlewich)
Lighterage Yard
Chester Way
Northwich CW8 5JT
Tel: Northwich (0606) 40566

British Waterways
Llangollen & Montgomery Canals
Ellesmere
Shropshire SY12 9AA
Tel: Ellesmere (0691) 622549

Acknowledgements

The front cover, based on the former Shropshire Union fleet livery is by Brian Collings. The back cover 'castle', based also on a traditional design, is by Jackie Pearson. The frontispiece, of "The Boat Inn" at Gnosall on the Shropshire Union Canal, together with all the other internal illustrations, are by Eric Leslie. We 'Heard it through the Grapevine' from: Toby Bryant and family, Richard J. Lightowler, N. Wilshaw, M.C. Temple, Douglas Mennear, and Keith Vigurs; thanks to them all for helping us stay 'up to date'. We are grateful, as always, to the staff of Characters and Penwell.

THE BEST HIRE CRUISERS ON THE CANALS
Central for the lovely
LLANGOLLEN & SHROPSHIRE UNION CANALS

ENGLISH COUNTY CRUISES
Colour brochures and bookings
Telephone: 0270 780544 (2 lines)
WRENBURY MILL, WRENBURY, near NANTWICH, Cheshire CW5 8HG
'A Friendly Family Company whose boats always look new'